D1133118

Christian Healing

———

The People's Idea of God

———

Pulpit and Press

———

Christian Science Versus
Pantheism

———

Message to The Mother
Church, 1900

———

Message to The Mother
Church, 1901

———

Message to The Mother
Church, 1902

Christian Healing

A Sermon Delivered at Boston

Christian Healing

A Sermon Delivered at Boston

by

Mary Baker Eddy

Discoverer and Founder of Christian Science
and Author of Science and Health with
Key to the Scriptures

Published by the
Trustees under the Will of Mary Baker G. Eddy
Boston, U.S.A.

Authorized Literature of
The First Church of Christ, Scientist
in Boston, Massachusetts

Sermon

SUBJECT

CHRISTIAN HEALING

TEXT: *And these signs shall follow them that believe; In my name* 1
shall they cast out devils; they shall speak with new tongues; they
shall take up serpents; and if they drink any deadly thing, it shall 3
not hurt them; they shall lay hands on the sick, and they shall recover.
— MARK XVI. 17, 18

HISTORY repeats itself; to-morrow grows out of to- 6
day. But Heaven's favors are formidable: they are
calls to higher duties, not discharge from care; and whoso
builds on less than an immortal basis, hath built on sand. 9

We have asked, in our selfishness, to wait until the age
advanced to a more practical and spiritual religion before
arguing with the world the great subject of Christian heal- 12
ing; but our answer was, "Then there were no cross to
take up, and less need of publishing the good news." A
classic writes, — 15

> "At thirty, man suspects himself a fool;
> Knows it at forty, and reforms his plan;
> At fifty, chides his infamous delay, 18
> Pushes his prudent purpose to resolve."

The difference between religions is, that one religion has a
more spiritual basis and tendency than the other; and 21

[1]

the religion nearest right is that one. The genius of Christianity is works more than words; a calm and stead-fast communion with God; a tumult on earth, — religious factions and prejudices arrayed against it, the synagogues as of old closed upon it, while it reasons with the storm, hurls the thunderbolt of truth, and stills the tempest of error; scourged and condemned at every advancing foot-step, afterwards pardoned and adopted, but never seen amid the smoke of battle. Said the intrepid reformer, Martin Luther: "I am weary of the world, and the world is weary of me; the parting will be easy." Said the more gentle Melanchthon: "Old Adam is too strong for young Melanchthon."

And still another Christian hero, ere he passed from his execution to a crown, added his testimony: "I have fought a good fight, . . . I have kept the faith." But Jesus, the model of infinite patience, said: "Come unto me, all ye that labor and are heavy laden, and I will give you rest." And he said this when bending beneath the malice of the world. But why should the world hate Jesus, the loved of the Father, the loved of Love? It was that his spirituality rebuked their carnality, and gave this proof of Christianity that religions had not given. Again, they knew it was not in the power of eloquence or a dead rite to cast out error and heal the sick. Past, present, future magnifies his name who built, on Truth, eternity's foundation stone, and sprinkled the altar of Love with perpetual incense.

Such Christianity requires neither hygiene nor drugs
wherewith to heal both mind and body; or, lacking these,
to show its helplessness. The primitive privilege of Christianity was to make men better, to cast out error, and heal
the sick. It was a proof, more than a profession thereof;
a demonstration, more than a doctrine. It was the foundation of right thinking and right acting, and must be
reestablished on its former basis. The stone which the
builders rejected must again become the head of the
corner. In proportion as the personal and material element stole into religion, it lost Christianity and the power
to heal; and the qualities of God as a person, instead of
the divine Principle that begets the quality, engrossed the
attention of the ages. In the original text the term *God*
was derived from the word *good*. Christ is the idea
of Truth; Jesus is the name of a man born in a remote
province of Judea, — Josephus alludes to several individuals by the name of Jesus. Therefore Christ Jesus was
an honorary title; it signified a "good man," which epithet the great goodness and wonderful works of our
Master more than merited. Because God is the Principle of
Christian healing, we must understand in part this divine
Principle, or we cannot demonstrate it in part.

The Scriptures declare that "God is Love, Truth, and
Life," — a trinity in unity; not three persons in one, but
three statements of one Principle. We cannot tell what is
the person of Truth, the body of the infinite, but we know
that the Principle is not the person, that the finite cannot

1 contain the infinite, that unlimited Mind cannot start from
a limited body. The infinite can neither go forth from,
3 return to, nor remain for a moment within limits. We
must give freer breath to thought before calculating the
results of an infinite Principle, — the effects of infinite
6 Love, the compass of infinite Life, the power of infinite
Truth. Clothing Deity with personality, we limit the action of God to the finite senses. We pray for God to re-
9 member us, even as we ask a person with softening of the
brain not to forget his daily cares. We ask infinite wisdom
to possess our finite sense, and forgive what He knows
12 deserves to be punished, and to bless what is unfit to be
blessed. We expect infinite Love to drop divinity long
enough to hate. We expect infinite Truth to mix with
15 error, and become finite for a season; and, after infinite
Spirit is forced in and out of matter for an indefinite period,
to show itself infinite again. We expect infinite Life to
18 become finite, and have an end; but, after a temporary
lapse, to begin anew as infinite Life, without beginning and
without end.

21   Friends, can we ever arrive at a proper conception of the
divine character, and gain a right idea of the Principle of
all that is right, with such self-evident contradictions?
24 God must be our model, or we have none; and if this
model is one thing at one time, and the opposite of it at
another, can we rely on our model? Or, having faith in it,
27 how can we demonstrate a changing Principle? We cannot: we shall be consistent with our inconsistent statement

of Deity, and so bring out our own erring finite sense of God, and of good and evil blending. While admitting that God is omnipotent, we shall be limiting His power at every point, — shall be saying He is beaten by certain kinds of food, by changes of temperature, the neglect of a bath, and so on. Phrenology will be saying the developments of the brain bias a man's character. Physiology will be saying, if a man has taken cold by doing good to his neighbor, God will punish him now for the cold, but he must wait for the reward of his good deed hereafter. One of our leading clergymen startles us by saying that "between Christianity and spiritualism, the question chiefly is concerning the trustworthiness of the communications, and not the doubt of their reality." Does any one think the departed are not departed, but are with us, although we have no evidence of the fact except sleight-of-hand and hallucination?

Such hypotheses ignore Biblical authority, obscure the one grand truth which is constantly covered, in one way or another, from our sight. This truth is, that we are to work out our own salvation, and to meet the responsibility of our own thoughts and acts; relying not on the person of God or the person of man to do our work for us, but on the apostle's rule, "I will show thee my faith by my works." This spiritualism would lead our lives to higher issues; it would purify, elevate, and consecrate man; it would teach him that "whatsoever a man soweth, that shall he also reap." The more spiritual we become

1 here, the more are we separated from the world; and
should this rule fail hereafter, and we grow more material,
3 and so come back to the world? When I was told the other
day, "People say you are a medium," pardon me if I
smiled. The pioneer of something new under the sun is
6 never hit: he cannot be; the opinions of people fly too
high or too low. From my earliest investigations of the
mental phenomenon named mediumship, I knew it was
9 misinterpreted, and I said it. The spiritualists abused me
for it then, and have ever since; but they take pleasure in
calling me a medium. I saw the impossibility, in Science,
12 of intercommunion between the so-called dead and the
living. When I learned how mind produces disease on the
body, I learned how it produces the manifestations ig-
15 norantly imputed to spirits. I saw how the mind's ideals
were evolved and made tangible; and it matters not
whether that ideal is a flower or a cancer, if the belief is
18 strong enough to manifest it. Man thinks he is a medium
of disease; that when he is sick, disease controls his body
to whatever manifestation we see. But the fact remains,
21 in metaphysics, that the mind of the individual only can
produce a result upon his body. The belief that produces
this result may be wholly unknown to the individual, be-
24 cause it is lying back in the unconscious thought, a latent
cause producing the effect we see.

　　"And these signs shall follow them that believe; In
27 my name shall they cast out devils." The word *devil*
comes from the Greek *diabolos;* in Hebrew it is *belial*, and

signifies "that which is good for nothing, lust," etc. The
signs referred to are the manifestations of the power of
Truth to cast out error; and, correcting error in thought,
it produces the harmonious effect on the body. "Them
that believe" signifies those who understand God's supremacy, — the power of Mind over matter. "The new
tongue" is the spiritual meaning as opposed to the material.
It is the language of Soul instead of the senses; it translates
matter into its original language, which is Mind, and gives
the spiritual instead of the material signification. It begins
with motive, instead of act, where Jesus formed his estimate; and there correcting the motive, it corrects the act
that results from the motive. The Science of Christianity
makes pure the fountain, in order to purify the stream. It
begins in mind to heal the body, the same as it begins in
motive to correct the act, and through which to judge of it.
The Master of metaphysics, reading the mind of the poor
woman who dropped her mite into the treasury, said,
"She hath cast in more than they all." Again, he charged
home a crime to mind, regardless of any outward act, and
sentenced it as our judges would not have done to-day.
Jesus knew that adultery is a crime, and *mind* is the crim-
inal. I wish the age was up to his understanding of these
two facts, so important to progress and Christianity.

"They shall take up serpents; and if they drink any
deadly thing, it shall not hurt them." This is an unquali-
fied statement of the duty and ability of Christians to heal
the sick; and it contains no argument for a creed or doc-

1 trine, it implies no necessity beyond the understanding of
God, and obedience to His government, that heals both
3 mind and body; God, — not a person to whom we should
pray to heal the sick, but the Life, Love, and Truth that
destroy error and death. Understanding the truth regard-
6 ing mind and body, knowing that Mind can master sickness as well as sin, and carrying out this government over
both and bringing out the results of this higher Chris-
9 tianity, we shall perceive the meaning of the context,
— "They shall lay hands on the sick, and they shall
recover."

12 The world is slow to perceive individual advancement;
but when it reaches the thought that has produced this,
then it is willing to be made whole, and no longer quarrels
15 with the individual. Plato did better; he said, "What
thou seest, that thou beest."

The mistaken views entertained of Deity becloud the
18 light of revelation, and suffocate reason by materialism.
When we understand that God is what the Scriptures have
declared, — namely, Life, Truth, and Love, — we shall
21 learn to reach heaven through Principle instead of a pardon; and this will make us honest and laborious, knowing
that we shall receive only what we have earned. Jesus
24 illustrated this by the parable of the husbandman. If we
work to become Christians as honestly and as directly
upon a divine Principle, and adhere to the rule of this
27 Principle as directly as we do to the rule of mathematics,
we shall be Christian Scientists, and do more than we are

now doing, and progress faster than we are now pro- 1
gressing. We should have no anxiety about what is or
what is not the person of God, if we understood the 3
Principle better and employed our thoughts more in demonstrating it. We are constantly thinking and talking
on the wrong side of the question. The less said or thought 6
of sin, sickness, or death, the better for mankind, morally
and physically. The greatest sinner and the most hopeless invalid think most of sickness and of sin; but, having 9
learned that this method has not saved them from either,
why do they go on thus, and their moral advisers talk for
them on the very subjects they would gladly discontinue to 12
bring out in their lives? Contending for the reality of
what should disappear is like furnishing fuel for the flames.
Is it a duty for any one to believe that "the curse causeless 15
cannot come"? Then it is a higher duty to know that
God never cursed man, His own image and likeness. God
never made a wicked man; and man made by God had not 18
a faculty or power underived from his Maker wherewith to
make himself wicked.

The only correct answer to the question, "Who is 21
the author of evil?" is the scientific statement that
evil is unreal; that God made all that was made, but
He never made sin or sickness, either an error of mind 24
or of body. Life in matter is a dream: sin, sickness,
and death are this dream. Life is Spirit; and when we
waken from the dream of life in matter, we shall learn this 27
grand truth of being. St. John saw the vision of life in

1 matter; and he saw it pass away, — an illusion. The
dragon that was wroth with the woman, and stood ready
3 "to devour the child as soon as it was born," was the vision
of envy, sensuality, and malice, ready to devour the idea
of Truth. But the beast bowed before the Lamb: it was
6 supposed to have fought the manhood of God, that Jesus
represented; but it fell before the womanhood of God,
that presented the highest ideal of Love. Let us re-
9 member that God — good — is omnipotent; therefore evil
is impotent. There is but one side to good, — it has no
evil side; there is but one side to reality, and that is the
12 good side.

God is All, and in all: that finishes the question of
a good and a bad side to existence. Truth is the real;
15 error is the unreal. You will gather the importance of
this saying, when sorrow seems to come, if you will look
on the bright side; for sorrow endureth but for the night,
18 and joy cometh with the light. Then will your sorrow be
a dream, and your waking the reality, even the triumph
of Soul over sense. If you wish to be happy, argue with
21 yourself on the side of happiness; take the side you wish
to carry, and be careful not to talk on both sides, or to
argue stronger for sorrow than for joy. You are the at-
24 torney for the case, and will win or lose according to your
plea.

As the mountain hart panteth for the water brooks, so
27 panteth my heart for the true fount and Soul's baptism.
Earth's fading dreams are empty streams, her fountains

play in borrowed sunbeams, her plumes are plucked from
the wings of vanity. Did we survey the cost of sublunary
joy, we then should gladly waken to see it was unreal. A
dream calleth itself a dreamer, but when the dream has
passed, man is seen wholly apart from the dream.

We are in the midst of a revolution; physics are yielding slowly to metaphysics; mortal mind rebels at its own
boundaries; weary of matter, it would catch the meaning
of Spirit. The only immortal superstructure is built on
Truth; her modest tower rises slowly, but it stands and is
the miracle of the hour, though it may seem to the age like
the great pyramid of Egypt, — a miracle in stone. The
fires of ancient proscription burn upon the altars of to-day;
he who has suffered from intolerance is the first to be intolerant. Homœopathy may not recover from the heel of
allopathy before lifting its foot against its neighbor, metaphysics, although homœopathy has laid the foundation
stone of mental healing; it has established this axiom,
"The less medicine the better," and metaphysics adds,
"until you arrive at no medicine." When you have
reached this high goal you have learned that proportionately as matter went out and Mind came in as the remedy,
was its potency. Metaphysics places all cause and cure
as mind; differing in this from homœopathy, where cause
and cure are supposed to be both mind and matter. Metaphysics requires mind imbued with Truth to heal the sick;
hence the Christianity of metaphysical healing, and this
excellence above other systems. The higher attenuations

1 of homœopathy contain no medicinal properties, and
thus it is found out that Mind instead of matter heals
3 the sick.

While the matter-physician feels the pulse, examines
the tongue, etc., to learn what matter is doing independent
6 of mind, when it is self-evident it can do nothing, the
metaphysician goes to the fount to govern the streams;
he diagnoses disease as mind, the basis of all action, and
9 cures it thus when matter cannot cure it, showing he was
right. Thus it was we discovered that all physical effects
originate in mind before they can become manifest as
12 matter; we learned from the Scripture and Christ's healing
that God, directly or indirectly, through His providence
or His laws, never made a man sick. When studying the
15 two hundred and sixty remedies of the Jahr, the characteristic peculiarities and the general and moral symptoms
requiring the remedy, we saw at once the concentrated
18 power of thought brought to bear on the pharmacy of
homœopathy, which made the infinitesimal dose effectual.
To prepare the medicine requires time and thought; you
21 cannot shake the poor drug without the involuntary
thought, "I am making you more powerful," and the
sequel proves it; the higher attenuations prove that the
24 power was the thought, for when the drug disappears by
your process the power remains, and homœopathists admit the higher attenuations are the most powerful. The
27 only objection to giving the unmedicated sugar is, it would
be dishonest and divide one's faith apparently between

matter and mind, and so weaken both points of action; 1
taking hold of both horns of the dilemma, we should work
at opposites and accomplish less on either side.   3

The pharmacy of homœopathy is reducing the one hun-
dredth part of a grain of medicine two thousand times,
shaking the preparation thirty times at every attenuation. 6
There is a moral to this medicine; the higher natures are
reached soonest by the higher attenuations, until the fact is
found out they have taken no medicine, and then the so- 9
called drug loses its power. We have attenuated a grain of
aconite until it was no longer aconite, then dropped into
a tumblerful of water a single drop of this harmless solu- 12
tion, and administering one teaspoonful of this water at
intervals of half an hour have cured the incipient stage of
fever. The highest attenuation we ever attained was to 15
leave the drug out of the question, using only the sugar of
milk; and with this original dose we cured an inveterate
case of dropsy. After these experiments you cannot be 18
surprised that we resigned the imaginary medicine altogether, and honestly employed Mind as the only curative
Principle.   21

What are the foundations of metaphysical healing?
Mind, divine Science, the truth of being that casts out
error and thus heals the sick. You can readily perceive 24
this mental system of healing is the antipode of mesmerism, Beelzebub. Mesmerism makes one disease while it is
supposed to cure another, and that one is worse than the 27
first; mesmerism is one lie getting the better of another,

1 and the bigger lie occupying the field for a period; it is the fight of beasts, in which the bigger animal beats the lesser;
3 in fine, much ado about nothing. Medicine will not arrive at the science of treating disease until disease is treated mentally and man is healed morally and physically. What
6 has physiology, hygiene, or physics done for Christianity but to obscure the divine Principle of healing and encourage faith in an opposite direction?

9   Great caution should be exercised in the choice of physicians. If you employ a medical practitioner, be sure he is a learned man and skilful; never trust yourself in the
12 hands of a quack. In proportion as a physician is enlightened and liberal is he equipped with Truth, and his efforts are salutary; ignorance and charlatanism are miserable
15 medical aids. Metaphysical healing includes infinitely more than merely to know that mind governs the body and the method of a mental practice. The preparation for a
18 metaphysical practitioner is the most arduous task I ever performed. You must first mentally educate and develop the spiritual sense or perceptive faculty by which one learns
21 the metaphysical treatment of disease; you must teach them how to learn, together with what they learn. I waited many years for a student to reach the ability to
24 teach; it included more than they understood.

     Metaphysical or divine Science reveals the Principle and method of perfection, — how to attain a mind in harmony
27 with God, in sympathy with all that is right and opposed to all that is wrong, and a body governed by this mind.

Christian Science repudiates the evidences of the senses
and rests upon the supremacy of God. Christian healing,
established upon this Principle, vindicates the omnipotence of the Supreme Being by employing no other remedy
than Truth, Life, and Love, understood, to heal all ills
that flesh is heir to. It places no faith in hygiene or drugs;
it reposes all faith in mind, in spiritual power divinely
directed. By rightly understanding the power of mind
over matter, it enables mind to govern matter, as it rises
to that supreme sense that shall "take up serpents" un-
harmed, and "if they drink any deadly thing, it shall not
hurt them." Christian Science explains to any one's perfect satisfaction the so-called miracles recorded in the
Bible. Ah! why should man deny all might to the divine
Mind, and claim another mind perpetually at war with this
Mind, when at the same time he calls God almighty and
admits in statement what he denies in proof? You pray
for God to heal you, but should you expect this when you
are acting oppositely to your prayer, trying everything else
besides God, and believe that sickness is something He
cannot reach, but medicine can? as if drugs were superior
to Deity.

The Scripture says, "Ye ask, and receive not, because
ye ask amiss;" and is it not asking amiss to pray for a
proof of divine power, that you have little or no faith in
because you do not understand God, the Principle of
this proof? Prayer will be inaudible, and works more
than words, as we understand God better. The Lord's

1 Prayer, understood in its spiritual sense, and given its
spiritual version, can never be repeated too often for the
3 benefit of all who, having ears, hear and understand.
Metaphysical Science teaches us there is no other Life,
substance, and intelligence but God. How much are you
6 demonstrating of this statement? which to you hath the
most actual substance, — wealth and fame, or Truth and
Love? See to it, O Christian Scientists, ye who have
9 named the name of Christ with a higher meaning, that you
abide by your statements, and abound in Love and Truth,
for unless you do this you are not demonstrating the
12 Science of metaphysical healing. The immeasurable
Life and Love will occupy your affections, come nearer
your hearts and into your homes when you touch but the
15 hem of Truth's garment.

A word about the five personal senses, and we will leave
our abstract subjects for this time. The only evidence we
18 have of sin, sickness, or death is furnished by these senses;
but how can we rely on their testimony when the senses
afford no evidence of Truth? They can neither see, hear,
21 feel, taste, nor smell God; and shall we call that reliable
evidence through which we can gain no understanding of
Truth, Life, and Love? Again, shall we say that God
24 hath created those senses through which it is impossible to
approach Him? Friends, it is of the utmost importance
that we look into these subjects, and gain our evidences of
27 Life from the correct source. Jesus said, "I am the way,
the truth, and the life. No man cometh unto the Father,

but by me," — through the footsteps of Truth. Not by the senses — the lusts of the flesh, the pride of life, envy, hypocrisy, or malice, the pleasures or the pains of the personal senses — does man get nearer his divine nature and present the image and likeness of God. How, then, can it be that material man and the personal senses were created by God? Love makes the spiritual man, lust makes the material so-called man, and God made all that was made; therefore the so-called material man and these personal senses, with all their evidences of sin, sickness, and death, are but a dream, — they are not the realities of life; and we shall all learn this as we awake to behold His likeness.

The allegory of Adam, when spiritually understood, explains this dream of material life, even the dream of the "deep sleep" that fell upon Adam when the spiritual senses were hushed by material sense that before had claimed audience with a serpent. Sin, sickness, and death never proceeded from Truth, Life, and Love. Sin, sickness, and death are error; they are not Truth, and therefore are not TRUE. Sin is a supposed mental condition; sickness and death are supposed physical ones, but all appeared through the false supposition of life and intelligence in matter. Sin was first in the allegory, and sickness and death were produced by sin. Then was not sin of mental origin, and did not mind originate the delusion? If sickness and death came through mind, so must they go; and are we not right in ruling them out of

1 mind to destroy their effects upon the body, that both
mortal mind and mortal body shall yield to the govern-
3 ment of God, immortal Mind? In the words of Paul,
that "the old man" shall be "put off," mortality shall
disappear and immortality be brought to light. People are
6 willing to put new wine into old bottles; but if this be
done, the bottle will break and the wine be spilled.

There is no connection between Spirit and matter.
9 Spirit never entered and it never escaped from matter;
good and evil never dwelt together. There is in reality
but the good: Truth is the real; error, the unreal. We
12 cannot put the new wine into old bottles. If that could be
done, the world would accept our sentiments; it would willingly adopt the new idea, if that idea could be reconciled
15 with the old belief; it would put the new wine into the
old bottle if it could prevent its effervescing and keep it
from popping out until it became popular.

18   The doctrine of atonement never did anything for sickness or claimed to reach that woe; but Jesus' mission
extended to the sick as much as to the sinner: he estab-
21 lished his Messiahship on the basis that Christ, Truth,
heals the sick. Pride, appetites, passions, envy, and malice
will cease to assert their Cæsar sway when metaphysics is
24 understood; and religion at the sick-bed will be no blind
Samson shorn of his locks. You must admit that what is
termed death has been produced by a belief alone. The
27 Oxford students proved this: they killed a man by no other
means than making him believe he was bleeding to death.

A felon was delivered to them for experiment to test the power of mind over body; and they did test it, and proved it. They proved it not in part, but as a whole; they proved that every organ of the system, every function of the body, is governed directly and entirely by mind, else those functions could not have been stopped by mind independently of material conditions. Had they changed the felon's belief that he was bleeding to death, removed the bandage from his eyes, and he had seen that a vein had not been opened, he would have resuscitated. The illusive origin of disease is not an exception to the origin of all mortal things. Spirit is causation, and the ancient question, Which is first, the egg or the bird? is answered by the Scripture, He made "every plant of the field before it was in the earth."

Heaven's signet is Love. We need it to stamp our religions and to spiritualize thought, motive, and endeavor. Tireless Being, patient of man's procrastination, affords him fresh opportunities every hour; but if Science makes a more spiritual demand, bidding man go up higher, he is impatient perhaps, or doubts the feasibility of the demand. But let us work more earnestly in His vineyard, and according to the model on the mount, bearing the cross meekly along the rugged way, into the wilderness, up the steep ascent, on to heaven, making our words golden rays in the sunlight of our deeds; and "these signs shall follow them that believe; . . . they shall lay hands on the sick, and they shall recover."

1 The following hymn was sung at the close: —

> "Oh, could we speak the matchless worth,
> 3 Oh, could we sound the glories forth,
> Which in our Saviour shine,
> We'd soar and touch the heavenly strings,
> 6 And vie with Gabriel, while he sings,
> In notes almost divine."

The People's Idea of God

Its Effect on

Health and Christianity

A Sermon Delivered at Boston

The
People's Idea of God

Its Effect on
Health and Christianity

A Sermon Delivered at Boston

by

Mary Baker Eddy

Discoverer and Founder of Christian Science
and Author of Science and Health with
Key to the Scriptures

Published by the
Trustees under the Will of Mary Baker G. Eddy
Boston, U.S.A.

Sermon

THE PEOPLE'S IDEA OF GOD

TEXT: *One Lord, one faith, one baptism.* — EPHESIANS iv. 5   1

EVERY step of progress is a step more spiritual. The great element of reform is not born of human wis-   3
dom; it draws not its life from human organizations; rather is it the crumbling away of material elements from reason, the translation of law back to its original language,   6
— Mind, and the final unity between man and God. The footsteps of thought, as they pass from the sensual side of existence to the reality and Soul of all things, are   9
slow, portending a long night to the traveller; but the guardians of the gloom are the angels of His presence, that impart grandeur to the intellectual wrestling and colli-   12
sions with old-time faiths, as we drift into more spiritual latitudes. The beatings of our heart can be heard; but the ceaseless throbbings and throes of thought are unheard,   15
as it changes from material to spiritual standpoints. Even the pangs of death disappear, accordingly as the under-standing that we are spiritual beings here reappears, and   18

1 we learn our capabilities for good, which insures man's
continuance and is the true glory of immortality.

3   The improved theory and practice of religion and of
medicine are mainly due to the people's improved views
of the Supreme Being. As the finite sense of Deity, based
6 on material conceptions of spiritual being, yields its grosser
elements, we shall learn what God is, and what God does.
The Hebrew term that gives another letter to the word
9 *God* and makes it *good*, unites Science and Christianity,
whereby we learn that God, good, is universal, and the
divine Principle, — Life, Truth, Love; and this Principle is
12 learned through goodness, and of Mind instead of matter,
of Soul instead of the senses, and by revelation supporting
reason. It is the false conceptions of Spirit, based on the
15 evidences gained from the material senses, that make a
Christian only in theory, shockingly material in practice,
and form its Deity out of the worst human qualities, else
18 of wood or stone.

Such a theory has overturned empires in demoniacal con-
tests over religion. Proportionately as the people's belief
21 of God, in every age, has been dematerialized and unfinited
has their Deity become good; no longer a personal tyrant
or a molten image, but the divine Life, Truth, and Love,
24 — Life without beginning or ending, Truth without a
lapse or error, and Love universal, infinite, eternal. This
more perfect idea, held constantly before the people's
27 mind, must have a benign and elevating influence upon
the character of nations as well as individuals, and will

lift man ultimately to the understanding that our ideals   1
form our characters, that as a man "thinketh in his heart,
so is he." The crudest ideals of speculative theology   3
have made monsters of men; and the ideals of *materia
medica* have made helpless invalids and cripples. The
eternal roasting amidst noxious vapors; the election of the   6
minority to be saved and the majority to be eternally punished; the wrath of God, to be appeased by the sacrifice
and torture of His favorite Son, — are some of the false   9
beliefs that have produced sin, sickness, and death; and
then would affirm that these are natural, and that Christianity and Christ-healing are preternatural; yea, that   12
make a mysterious God and a natural devil.

Let us rejoice that the bow of omnipotence already
spans the moral heavens with light, and that the more   15
spiritual idea of good and Truth meets the old material
thought like a promise upon the cloud, while it inscribes
on the thoughts of men at this period a more metaphysical   18
religion founded upon Christian Science. A personal
God is based on finite premises, where thought begins
wrongly to apprehend the infinite, even the quality or the   21
quantity of eternal good. This limited sense of God as
good limits human thought and action in their goodness,
and assigns them mortal fetters in the outset. It has im-   24
planted in our religions certain unspiritual shifts, such as
dependence on personal pardon for salvation, rather than
obedience to our Father's demands, whereby we grow out   27
of sin in the way that our Lord has appointed; namely,

1 by working out our own salvation. It has given to all
systems of *materia medica* nothing but materialism, —
3 more faith in hygiene and drugs than in God. Idolatry
sprang from the belief that God is a form, more than an
infinite and divine Mind; sin, sickness, and death origi-
6 nated in the belief that Spirit materialized into a body,
infinity became finity, or man, and the eternal entered the
temporal. Mythology, or the myth of ologies, said that
9 Life, which is infinite and eternal, could enter finite man
through his nostrils, and matter become intelligent of
good and evil, because a serpent said it. When first good,
12 God, was named a person, and evil another person, the
error that a personal God and a personal devil entered
into partnership and would form a third person, called
15 material man, obtained expression. But these unspiritual and mysterious ideas of God and man are far from
correct.
18   The glorious Godhead is Life, Truth, and Love, and
these three terms for one divine Principle are the three in
one that can be understood, and that find no reflection in
21 sinning, sick, and dying mortals. No miracle of grace can
make a spiritual mind out of beliefs that are as material as
the heathen deities. The pagan priests appointed Apollo
24 and Esculapius the gods of medicine, and they inquired of
these heathen deities what drugs to prescribe. Systems
of religion and of medicine grown out of such false ideals
27 of the Supreme Being cannot heal the sick and cast out
devils, error. Eschewing a materialistic and idolatrous

theory and practice of medicine and religion, the apostle 1
devoutly recommends the more spiritual Christianity, —
"one Lord, one faith, one baptism." The prophets and 3
apostles, whose lives are the embodiment of a living faith,
have not taken away our Lord, that we know not where they
have laid him; they have resurrected a deathless life of 6
love; and into the cold materialisms of dogma and doctrine
we look in vain for their more spiritual ideal, the risen
Christ, whose *materia medica* and theology were one. 9

The ideals of primitive Christianity are nigh, even at
our door. Truth is not lost in the mists of remoteness or
the barbarisms of spiritless codes. The right ideal is not 12
buried, but has risen higher to our mortal sense, and
having overcome death and the grave, wrapped in a pure
winding-sheet, it sitteth beside the sepulchre in angel 15
form, saying unto us, "Life is God; and our ideal of God
has risen above the sod to declare His omnipotence." This
white-robed thought points away from matter and doc- 18
trine, or dogma, to the diviner sense of Life and Love, —
yea, to the Principle that is God, and to the demonstration thereof in healing the sick. Let us then heed this heav- 21
enly visitant, and not entertain the angel unawares.

The ego is not self-existent matter animated by mind,
but in itself is mind; therefore a Truth-filled mind makes 24
a pure Christianity and a healthy mind and body. Oliver
Wendell Holmes said, in a lecture before the Harvard
Medical School: "I firmly believe that if the whole *materia* 27
medica could be sunk to the bottom of the sea, it would be

1 all the better for mankind and all the worse for the fishes."
Dr. Benjamin Waterhouse writes: "I am sick of learned
3 quackery." Dr. Abercrombie, Fellow of the Royal College of Physicians in Edinburgh, writes: "Medicine is the
science of guessing." Dr. James Johnson, Surgeon Ex-
6 traordinary to the King, says: "I declare my conscientious
belief, founded on long observation and reflection, that
if there was not a single physician, surgeon, apothecary,
9 man-midwife, chemist, druggist, or drug on the face of
the earth, there would be less sickness and less mortality
than now obtains." Voltaire says: "The art of medicine
12 consists in amusing the patient while nature cures the
disease."

Believing that man is the victim of his Maker, we natu-
15 rally fear God more than we love Him; whereas "perfect
Love casteth out fear;" but when we learn God aright, we
love Him, because He is found altogether lovely. Thus it
18 is that a more spiritual and true ideal of Deity improves
the race physically and spiritually. God is no longer a
mystery to the Christian Scientist, but a divine Principle,
21 understood in part, because the grand realities of Life and
Truth are found destroying sin, sickness, and death; and
it should no longer be deemed treason to understand God,
24 when the Scriptures enjoin us to "acquaint now thyself
with Him [God], and be at peace;" we should understand
something of that great good for which we are to leave all
27 else.

Periods and peoples are characterized by their highest

or their lowest ideals, by their God and their devil. We are 1
all sculptors, working out our own ideals, and leaving the
impress of mind on the body as well as on history and 3
marble, chiselling to higher excellence, or leaving to rot and
ruin the mind's ideals. Recognizing this as we ought, we
shall turn often from marble to model, from matter to 6
Mind, to beautify and exalt our lives.

"Chisel in hand stood a sculptor-boy,
  With his marble block before him; 9
And his face lit up with a smile of joy
  As an angel dream passed o'er him.
He carved the dream on that shapeless stone 12
  With many a sharp incision.
With heaven's own light the sculptor shone, —
  He had caught the angel-vision. 15

"Sculptors of life are we as we stand
  With our lives uncarved before us,
Waiting the hour when at God's command 18
  Our life dream passes o'er us.
If we carve it then on the yielding stone
  With many a sharp incision, 21
Its heavenly beauty shall be our own, —
  Our lives that angel-vision."

To remove those objects of sense called sickness and dis- 24
ease, we must appeal to mind to improve its subjects and
objects of thought, and give to the body those better de-
lineations. Scientific discovery and the inspiration of 27
Truth have taught me that the health and character of
man become more or less perfect as his mind-models are
more or less spiritual. Because God is Spirit, our thoughts 30
must spiritualize to approach Him, and our methods grow
more spiritual to accord with our thoughts. Religion and

1 medicine must be dematerialized to present the right idea
of Truth; then will this idea cast out error and heal the
3 sick. If changeableness that repenteth itself; partiality
that elects some to be saved and others to be lost, or that
answers the prayer of one and not of another; if incom-
6 petency that cannot heal the sick, or lack of love that will
not; if unmercifulness, that for the sins of a few tired
years punishes man eternally, — are our conceptions of
9 Deity, we shall bring out these qualities of character in our
own lives and extend their influence to others.

Judaism, enjoining the limited and definite form of a
12 national religion, was not more the antithesis of Christianity than are our finite and material conceptions of
Deity. Life is God; but we say that Life is carried on
15 through principal processes, and speculate concerning
material forces. Mind is supreme; and yet we make more
of matter, and lean upon it for health and life. Mind,
18 that governs the universe, governs every action of the body
as directly as it moves a planet and controls the muscles
of the arm. God grant that the trembling chords of human
21 hope shall again be swept by the divine *Talitha cumi*,
"Damsel, I say unto thee, arise." Then shall Christian
Science again appear, to light our sepulchres with im-
24 mortality. We thank our Father that to-day the uncre-
mated fossils of material systems, already charred, are
fast fading into ashes; and that man will ere long stop
27 trusting where there is no trust, and gorging his faith with
skill proved a million times unskilful.

Christian Science has one faith, one Lord, one baptism; 1
and this faith builds on Spirit, not matter; and this baptism is the purification of mind, — not an ablution of the 3
body, but tears of repentance, an overflowing love, washing away the motives for sin; yea, it is love leaving self
for God. The cool bath may refresh the body, or as com- 6
pliance with a religious rite may declare one's belief; but
it cannot purify his mind, or meet the demands of Love.
It is the baptism of Spirit that washes our robes and makes 9
them white in the blood of the Lamb; that bathes us in the
life of Truth and the truth of Life. Having one Lord, we
shall not be idolaters, dividing our homage and obedience 12
between matter and Spirit; but shall work out our own
salvation, after the model of our Father, who never par-
dons the sin that deserves to be punished and can be de- 15
stroyed only through suffering.

We ask and receive not, because we "ask amiss;" even
dare to invoke the divine aid of Spirit to heal the sick, and 18
then administer drugs with full confidence in their efficacy,
showing our greater faith in matter, despite the authority
of Jesus that "ye cannot serve two masters." 21

Silent prayer is a desire, fervent, importunate: here
metaphysics is seen to rise above physics, and rest all faith
in Spirit, and remove all evidence of any other power than 24
Mind; whereby we learn the great fact that there is no
omnipotence, unless omnipotence is the *All*-power. This
truth of Deity, understood, destroys discord with the higher 27
and more potent evidences in Christian Science of man's

1 harmony and immortality. Thought is the essence of an
act, and the stronger element of action; even as steam is
3 more powerful than water, simply because it is more
ethereal. Essences are refinements that lose some materiality; and as we struggle through the cold night of physics,
6 matter will become vague, and melt into nothing under the
microscope of Mind.

Massachusetts succored a fugitive slave in 1853, and put
9 her humane foot on a tyrannical prohibitory law regulating
the practice of medicine in 1880. It were well if the sister
States had followed her example and sustained as nobly
12 our constitutional Bill of Rights. Discerning the God-
given rights of man, Paul said, "I was free born." Justice
and truth make man free, injustice and error enslave
15 him. Mental Science alone grasps the standard of liberty,
and battles for man's whole rights, divine as well as human. It assures us, of a verity, that mortal beliefs, and
18 not a law of nature, have made men sinning and sick, —
that they alone have fettered free limbs, and marred in
mind the model of man.

21 We possess our own body, and make it harmonious or
discordant according to the images that thought reflects
upon it. The emancipation of our bodies from sickness
24 will follow the mind's freedom from sin; and, as St. Paul
admonishes, we should be "waiting for the adoption, to
wit, the redemption of our body." The rights of man were
27 vindicated but in a single instance when African slavery
was abolished on this continent, yet that hour was a

prophecy of the full liberty of the sons of God as found in 1
Christian Science. The defenders of the rights of the
colored man were scarcely done with their battles before a 3
new abolitionist struck the keynote of higher claims, in
which it was found that the feeblest mind, enlightened
and spiritualized, can free its body from disease as well as 6
sin; and this victory is achieved, not with bayonet and
blood, not by inhuman warfare, but in divine peace.

Above the platform of human rights let us build another 9
staging for diviner claims, — even the supremacy of Soul
over sense, wherein man cooperates with and is made subject to his Maker. The lame, the blind, the sick, the sen- 12
sual, are slaves, and their fetters are gnawing away life
and hope; their chains are clasped by the false teachings,
false theories, false fears, that enforce new forms of op- 15
pression, and are the modern Pharaohs that hold the children of Israel still in bondage. Mortals, *alias* mortal
minds, make the laws that govern their bodies, as directly 18
as men pass legislative acts and enact penal codes; while
the body, obedient to the legislation of mind, but ignorant
of the law of belief, calls its own enactments "laws of 21
matter." The legislators who are greatly responsible for
all the woes of mankind are those leaders of public thought
who are mistaken in their methods of humanity. 24

The learned quacks of this period "bind heavy bur-
dens," that they themselves will not touch "with one of
their fingers." Scientific guessing conspires unwittingly 27
against the liberty and lives of men. Should we but

1 hearken to the higher law of God, we should think for one
moment of these divine statutes of God: Let them have
3 "dominion over all the earth." "And if they drink any
deadly thing, it shall not hurt them; they shall lay hands
on the sick, and they shall recover." The only law of sick-
6 ness or death is a law of mortal belief, an infringement
on the merciful and just government of God. When this
great fact is understood, the spurious, imaginary laws of
9 matter — when matter is not a lawgiver — will be dis-
puted and trampled under the feet of Truth. Deal, then,
with this fabulous law as with an inhuman State law; re-
12 peal it in mind, and acknowledge only God in all thy ways,
— "who forgiveth all thine iniquities; who healeth all thy
diseases." Few there be who know what a power mind is
15 to heal when imbued with the spiritual truth that lifts man
above the demands of matter.

As our ideas of Deity advance to truer conceptions,
18 we shall take in the remaining two thirds of God's plan
of redemption, — namely, man's salvation from sickness
and death. Our blessed Master demonstrated this great
21 truth of healing the sick and raising the dead as God's
whole plan, and proved the application of its Principle to
human wants. Having faith in drugs and hygienic drills,
24 we lose faith in omnipotence, and give the healing power
to matter instead of Spirit. As if Deity would not if He
could, or could not if He would, give health to man; when
27 our Father bestows heaven not more willingly than health;
for without health there could be no heaven.

The worshippers of wood and stone have a more mate- 1
rial deity, hence a lower order of humanity, than those
who believe that God is a personal Spirit. But the wor- 3
shippers of a person have a lower order of Christianity than
he who understands that the Divine Being is more than a
person, and can demonstrate in part this great impersonal 6
Life, Truth, and Love, casting out error and healing the
sick. This all-important understanding is gained in
Christian Science, revealing the one God and His all- 9
power and ever-presence, and the brotherhood of man in
unity of Mind and oneness of Principle.

On the startled ear of humanity rings out the iron tread 12
of merciless invaders, putting man to the rack for his
conscience, or forcing from the lips of manhood shameful
confessions, — Galileo kneeling at the feet of priestcraft, 15
and giving the lie to science. But the lofty faith of the
pious Polycarp proved the triumph of mind over the body,
when they threatened to let loose the wild beasts upon him, 18
and he replied: "Let them come; I cannot change at once
from good to bad." Then they bound him to the stake,
set fire to the fagots, and his pure faith went up through 21
the baptism of fire to a higher sense of Life. The infidel
was blind who said, "Christianity is fit only for women and
weak-minded men." But infidels disagree; for Bonaparte 24
said: "Since ever the history of Christianity was written,
the loftiest intellects have had a practical faith in God;"
and Daniel Webster said: "My heart has assured and re- 27
assured me that Christianity must be a divine reality."

1   As our ideas of Deity become more spiritual, we express them by objects more beautiful. To-day we clothe our
3 thoughts of death with flowers laid upon the bier, and in our cemeteries with amaranth blossoms, evergreen leaves, fragrant recesses, cool grottos, smiling fountains, and
6 white monuments. The dismal gray stones of church-yards have crumbled into decay, as our ideas of Life have grown more spiritual; and in place of "bat and owl on the
9 bending stones, are wreaths of immortelles, and white fingers pointing upward." Thus it is that our ideas of divinity form our models of humanity. O Christian Scien-
12 tist, thou of the church of the new-born; awake to a higher and holier love for God and man; put on the whole armor of Truth; rejoice in hope; be patient in tribulation,
15 — that ye may go to the bed of anguish, and look upon this dream of life in matter, girt with a higher sense of omnipo-tence; and behold once again the power of divine Life and
18 Love to heal and reinstate man in God's own image and likeness, having "one Lord, one faith, one baptism."

Pulpit and Press

Pulpit and Press

by

Mary Baker Eddy

Discoverer and Founder of Christian Science
and Author of Science and Health with
Key to the Scriptures

Published by the
Trustees under the Will of Mary Baker G. Eddy
Boston, U. S. A.

Preface

THIS volume contains scintillations from press and
pulpit — utterances which epitomize the story of the
birth of Christian Science, in 1866, and its progress
during the ensuing thirty years. Three quarters of a
century hence, when the children of to-day are the elders
of the twentieth century, it will be interesting to have
not only a record of the inclination given their own
thoughts in the latter half of the nineteenth century,
but also a registry of the rise of the mercury in the glass
of the world's opinion.

It will then be instructive to turn backward the tele-
scope of that advanced age, with its lenses of more
spiritual mentality, indicating the gain of intellectual
momentum, on the early footsteps of Christian Science
as planted in the pathway of this generation; to note
the impetus thereby given to Christianity; to con the
facts surrounding the cradle of this grand verity — that
the sick are healed and sinners saved, not by matter, but
by Mind; and to scan further the features of the vast
problem of eternal life, as expressed in the absolute
power of Truth and the actual bliss of man's existence
in Science.

MARY BAKER EDDY

February, 1895

Contents

Pulpit and Press

DEDICATORY SERMON

By Rev. Mary Baker Eddy

First Pastor of The First Church of Christ, Scientist, Boston, Mass.
Delivered January 6, 1895

Text: *They shall be abundantly satisfied with the fatness of Thy* 1
house; and Thou shalt make them drink of the river of Thy pleasures.
— Psalms xxxvi. 8.

3

A NEW year is a nursling, a babe of time, a prophecy
and promise clad in white raiment, kissed — and
encumbered with greetings — redolent with grief and 6
gratitude.

An old year is time's adult, and 1893 was a distinguished
character, notable for good and evil. Time past and time 9
present, both, may pain us, but time *improved* is eloquent in God's praise. For due refreshment garner the
memory of 1894; for if wiser by reason of its large lessons, 12
and records deeply engraven, great is the value thereof.

Pass on, returnless year!
The path behind thee is with glory crowned;   15
This spot whereon thou troddest was holy ground;
Pass proudly to thy bier!

To-day, being with you in spirit, what need that I should 18
be present *in propria persona?* Were I present, methinks

[1]

1 I should be much like the Queen of Sheba, when she saw
the house Solomon had erected. In the expressive language
3 of Holy Writ, "There was no more spirit in her;" and
she said, "Behold, the half was not told me: thy wisdom
and prosperity exceedeth the fame which I heard." Both
6 without and within, the spirit of beauty dominates The
Mother Church, from its mosaic flooring to the soft shimmer of its starlit dome.

9   Nevertheless, there is a thought higher and deeper than
the edifice. Material light and shade are temporal, not
eternal. Turning the attention from sublunary views,
12 however enchanting, think for a moment with me of the
house wherewith "they shall be abundantly satisfied," —
even the "house not made with hands, eternal in the
15 heavens." With the mind's eye glance at the direful
scenes of the war between China and Japan. Imagine
yourselves in a poorly barricaded fort, fiercely besieged
18 by the enemy. Would you rush forth single-handed to
combat the foe? Nay, would you not rather strengthen
your citadel by every means in your power, and remain
21 within the walls for its defense? Likewise should we do
as metaphysicians and Christian Scientists. The real
house in which "we live, and move, and have our being"
24 is Spirit, God, the eternal harmony of infinite Soul. The
enemy we confront would overthrow this sublime fortress,
and it behooves us to defend our heritage.

27   How can we do this Christianly scientific work? By
intrenching ourselves in the knowledge that our true
temple is no human fabrication, but the superstructure
30 of Truth, reared on the foundation of Love, and pinnacled

in Life. Such being its nature, how can our godly temple 1
possibly be demolished, or even disturbed? Can eternity
end? Can Life die? Can Truth be uncertain? Can 3
Love be less than boundless? Referring to this temple,
our Master said: "Destroy this temple, and in three days
I will raise it up." He also said: "The kingdom of God 6
is within you." Know, then, that you possess sovereign
power to think and act rightly, and that nothing can dis-
possess you of this heritage and trespass on Love. If you 9
maintain this position, who or what can cause you to sin
or suffer? Our surety is in our confidence that we are
indeed dwellers in Truth and Love, man's eternal mansion. 12
Such a heavenly assurance ends all warfare, and bids tumult cease, for the good fight we have waged is over, and
divine Love gives us the true sense of victory. "They 15
shall be abundantly satisfied with the fatness of Thy house;
and Thou shalt make them drink of the river of Thy
pleasures." No longer are we of the church militant, but 18
of the church triumphant; and with Job of old we ex-
claim, "Yet in my flesh shall I see God." The river of
His pleasures is a tributary of divine Love, whose living 21
waters have their source in God, and flow into everlasting
Life. We drink of this river when all human desires are
quenched, satisfied with what is pleasing to the divine 24
Mind.

Perchance some one of you may say, "The evidence of
spiritual verity in me is so small that I am afraid. I feel 27
so far from victory over the flesh that to reach out for a
present realization of my hope savors of temerity. Because of my own unfitness for such a spiritual animus my 30

1 strength is naught and my faith fails." O thou "weak
and infirm of purpose." Jesus said, "Be not afraid"!

3   "What if the little rain should say,
                    'So small a drop as I
                Can ne'er refresh a drooping earth,
6   I'll tarry in the sky.'"

Is not a man metaphysically and mathematically number one, a unit, and therefore whole number, governed
9 and protected by his divine Principle, God? You have
simply to preserve a scientific, positive sense of unity with
your divine source, and daily demonstrate this. Then you
12 will find that one is as important a factor as duodecillions
in being and doing right, and thus demonstrating deific
Principle. A dewdrop reflects the sun. Each of Christ's
15 little ones reflects the infinite One, and therefore is the
seer's declaration true, that "one on God's side is a
majority."

18 A single drop of water may help to hide the stars, or
crown the tree with blossoms.

Who lives in good, lives also in God, — lives in all Life,
21 through all space. His is an individual kingdom, his diadem a crown of crowns. His existence is deathless, forever unfolding its eternal Principle. Wait patiently on
24 illimitable Love, the lord and giver of Life. *Reflect this
Life*, and with it cometh the full power of being. "They
shall be abundantly satisfied with the fatness of Thy
27 house."

In 1893 the World's Parliament of Religions, held in
Chicago, used, in all its public sessions, my form of prayer

since 1866; and one of the very clergymen who had pub- 1
licly proclaimed me "the prayerless Mrs. Eddy," offered
his audible adoration in the words I use, besides listening 3
to an address on Christian Science from my pen, read by
Judge S. J. Hanna, in that unique assembly.

When the light of one friendship after another passes 6
from earth to heaven, we kindle in place thereof the glow
of some deathless reality. Memory, faithful to goodness,
holds in her secret chambers those characters of holiest 9
sort, bravest to endure, firmest to suffer, soonest to renounce. Such was the founder of the Concord School of
Philosophy — the late A. Bronson Alcott. 12

After the publication of "Science and Health with Key
to the Scriptures," his athletic mind, scholarly and serene,
was the first to bedew my hope with a drop of humanity. 15
When the press and pulpit cannonaded this book, he
introduced himself to its author by saying, "I have come
to comfort you." Then eloquently paraphrasing it, and 18
prophesying its prosperity, his conversation with a beauty
all its own reassured me. *That prophecy is fulfilled.*

This book, in 1895, is in its ninety-first edition of one 21
thousand copies. It is in the public libraries of the principal cities, colleges, and universities of America; also
the same in Great Britain, France, Germany, Russia, 24
Italy, Greece, Japan, India, and China; in the Oxford
University and the Victoria Institute, England; in the
Academy of Greece, and the Vatican at Rome. 27

This book is the leaven fermenting religion; it is
palpably working in the sermons, Sunday Schools, and
literature of our and other lands. This spiritual chemi- 30

1 calization is the upheaval produced when Truth is neutral-
izing error and impurities are passing off. And it will
3 continue till the antithesis of Christianity, engendering the
limited forms of a national or tyrannical religion, yields to
the church established by the Nazarene Prophet and main-
6 tained on the spiritual foundation of Christ's healing.

Good, the Anglo-Saxon term for God, unites Science to
Christianity. It presents to the understanding, not matter,
9 but Mind; not the deified drug, but the goodness of God —
healing and saving mankind.

The author of "Marriage of the Lamb," who made the
12 mistake of thinking she caught her notions from my book,
wrote to me in 1894, "Six months ago your book, Science
and Health, was put into my hands. I had not read three
15 pages before I realized I had found that for which I had
hungered since girlhood, and was healed instantaneously
of an ailment of seven years' standing. I cast from me the
18 false remedy I had vainly used, and turned to the 'great
Physician.' I went with my husband, a missionary to
China, in 1884. He went out under the auspices of the
21 Methodist Episcopal Church. I feel the truth is leading
us to return to Japan."

Another brilliant enunciator, seeker, and servant of
24 Truth, the Rev. William R. Alger of Boston, signalled
me kindly as my lone bark rose and fell and rode the rough
sea. At a *conversazione* in Boston, he said, "You may
27 find in Mrs. Eddy's metaphysical teachings more than is
dreamt of in your philosophy."

Also that renowned apostle of anti-slavery, Wendell
30 Phillips, the native course of whose mind never swerved

from the chariot-paths of justice, speaking of my work, said: "Had I young blood in my veins, I would help that woman."

I love Boston, and especially the laws of the State whereof this city is the capital. To-day, as of yore, her laws have befriended progress.

Yet when I recall the past, — how the gospel of healing was simultaneously praised and persecuted in Boston, — and remember also that God is just, I wonder whether, were our dear Master in our New England metropolis at this hour, he would not weep over it, as he wept over Jerusalem! O ye tears! Not in vain did ye flow. Those sacred drops were but enshrined for future use, and God has now unsealed their receptacle with His outstretched arm. Those crystal globes made morals for mankind. They will rise with joy, and with power to wash away, in floods of forgiveness, every crime, even when mistakenly committed in the name of religion.

An unjust, unmerciful, and oppressive priesthood must perish, for false prophets in the present as in the past stumble onward to their doom; while their tabernacles crumble with dry rot. "God is not mocked," and "the word of the Lord endureth forever."

I have ordained the Bible and the Christian Science textbook, "Science and Health with Key to the Scriptures," as pastor of The First Church of Christ, Scientist, in Boston, — so long as this church is satisfied with this pastor. This is my first ordination. "They shall be abundantly satisfied with the fatness of Thy house; and Thou shalt make them drink of the river of Thy pleasures."

All praise to the press of America's Athens, — and throughout our land the press has spoken out historically, impartially. Like the winds telling tales through the leaves of an ancient oak, unfallen, may our church chimes repeat my thanks to the press.

Notwithstanding the perplexed condition of our nation's finances, the want and woe with millions of dollars unemployed in our money centres, the Christian Scientists, within fourteen months, responded to the call for this church with $191,012. Not a mortgage was given nor a loan solicited, and the donors all touchingly told their privileged joy at helping to build The Mother Church. There was no urging, begging, or borrowing; only the need made known, and forth came the money, or diamonds, which served to erect this "miracle in stone."

Even the children vied with their parents to meet the demand. Little hands, never before devoted to menial services, shoveled snow, and babes gave kisses to earn a few pence toward this consummation. Some of these lambs my prayers had christened, but Christ will rechristen them with his own new name. "Out of the mouths of babes and sucklings Thou hast perfected praise." The resident youthful workers were called "Busy Bees."

Sweet society, precious children, your loving hearts and deft fingers distilled the nectar and painted the finest flowers in the fabric of this history, — even its centre-piece, — Mother's Room in The First Church of Christ, Scientist, in Boston. The children are destined to witness results which will eclipse Oriental dreams. They belong to the twentieth century. By juvenile aid, into the build-

ing fund have come $4,460.[1] Ah, children, you are the
bulwarks of freedom, the cement of society, the hope of
our race!

Brothers of the Christian Science Board of Directors,
when your tireless tasks are done — well done — no Delphian lyre could break the full chords of such a rest. May
the altar you have built never be shattered in our hearts,
but justice, mercy, and love kindle perpetually its fires.

It was well that the brother whose appliances warm
this house, warmed also our perishless hope, and nerved
its grand fulfilment. Woman, true to her instinct, came
to the rescue as sunshine from the clouds; so, when man
quibbled over an architectural exigency, a woman climbed
with feet and hands to the top of the tower, and helped
settle the subject.

After the loss of our late lamented pastor, Rev. D. A.
Easton, the church services were maintained by excellent
sermons from the editor of *The Christian Science Journal*
(who, with his better half, is a very whole man), together
with the Sunday School giving this flock "drink from the
river of His pleasures." O glorious hope and blessed assurance, "it is your Father's good pleasure to give you the
kingdom." Christians rejoice in secret, they have a bounty
hidden from the world. Self-forgetfulness, purity, and
love are treasures untold — constant prayers, prophecies,
and anointings. Practice, not profession, — goodness, not
doctrines, — spiritual understanding, not mere belief,
gain the ear and right hand of omnipotence, and call down
blessings infinite. "Faith without works is dead." The
foundation of enlightened faith is Christ's teachings and

[1] This sum was increased to $5,568.51 by contributions which reached the Treasurer after the Dedicatory Services.

1 *practice.* It was our Master's self-immolation, his life-giving love, healing both mind and body, that raised the
3 deadened conscience, paralyzed by inactive faith, to a quickened sense of mortal's necessities, — and God's power and purpose to supply them. It was, in the words
6 of the Psalmist, He "who forgiveth all thine iniquities; who healeth all thy diseases."

Rome's fallen fanes and silent Aventine is glory's tomb;
9 her pomp and power lie low in dust. Our land, more favored, had its Pilgrim Fathers. On shores of solitude, at Plymouth Rock, they planted a nation's heart, — the
12 rights of conscience, imperishable glory. No dream of avarice or ambition broke their exalted purpose, theirs was the wish to reign in hope's reality — the realm of
15 Love.

Christian Scientists, you have planted your standard on the rock of Christ, the true, the spiritual idea, — the
18 chief corner-stone in the house of our God. And our Master said: "The stone which the builders rejected, the same is become the head of the corner." If you are less
21 appreciated to-day than your forefathers, wait — for if you are as devout as they, and more scientific, as progress certainly demands, your plant is immortal. Let us rejoice
24 that chill vicissitudes have not withheld the timely shelter of this house, which descended like day-spring from on high.

27 Divine presence, breathe Thou Thy blessing on every heart in this house. Speak out, O soul! This is the new-born of Spirit, this is His redeemed; this, His beloved.
30 May the kingdom of God within you, — with you alway, —

reascending, bear you outward, upward, heavenward. 1
May the sweet song of silver-throated singers, making
melody more real, and the organ's voice, as the sound of 3
many waters, and the Word spoken in this sacred temple
dedicated to the ever-present God — mingle with the joy
of angels and rehearse your hearts' holy intents. May all 6
whose means, energies, and prayers helped erect The
Mother Church, find within it home, and *heaven*.

1   The following selections from "Science and Health
with Key to the Scriptures," pages 568–571, were read
3 from the platform. The impressive stillness of the audience indicated close attention.

    Revelation xii. 10–12. And I heard a loud voice saying in
6 heaven, Now is come salvation, and strength, and the kingdom of our God, and the power of His Christ: for the accuser
of our brethren is cast down, which accused them before our
9 God day and night. And they overcame him by the blood
of the Lamb, and by the word of their testimony; and they
loved not their lives unto the death. Therefore rejoice, ye
12 heavens, and ye that dwell in them. Woe to the inhabiters
of the earth and of the sea! for the devil is come down unto
you, having great wrath, because he knoweth that he hath
15 but a short time.

    For victory over a single sin, we give thanks and mag-
nify the Lord of Hosts. What shall we say of the mighty
18 conquest over all sin? A louder song, sweeter than has
ever before reached high heaven, now rises clearer and
nearer to the great heart of Christ; for the accuser is not
21 there, and Love sends forth her primal and everlasting
strain. Self-abnegation, by which we lay down all for
Truth, or Christ, in our warfare against error, is a rule in
24 Christian Science. This rule clearly interprets God as

divine Principle, — as Life, represented by the Father; 1
as Truth, represented by the Son; as Love, represented
by the Mother. Every mortal at some period, here or here- 3
after, must grapple with and overcome the mortal belief
in a power opposed to God.

The Scripture, "Thou hast been faithful over a few 6
things, I will make thee ruler over many," is literally fulfilled, when we are conscious of the supremacy of Truth,
by which the nothingness of error is seen; and we know 9
that the nothingness of error is in proportion to its wickedness. He that touches the hem of Christ's robe and masters
his mortal beliefs, animality, and hate, rejoices in the proof 12
of healing, — in a sweet and certain sense that God is
Love. Alas for those who break faith with divine Science
and fail to strangle the serpent of sin as well as of sickness! 15
They are dwellers still in the deep darkness of belief.
They are in the surging sea of error, not struggling to lift
their heads above the drowning wave. 18

What must the end be? They must eventually expiate
their sin through suffering. The sin, which one has made
his bosom companion, comes back to him at last with 21
accelerated force, for the devil knoweth his time is short.
Here the Scriptures declare that evil is temporal, not
eternal. The dragon is at last stung to death by his own 24
malice; but how many periods of torture it may take to
remove all sin, must depend upon sin's obduracy.

Revelation xii. 13. And when the dragon saw that he was 27
cast unto the earth, he persecuted the woman which brought
forth the man child.

1 The march of mind and of honest investigation will
bring the hour when the people will chain, with fetters of
3 some sort, the growing occultism of this period. The
present apathy as to the tendency of certain active yet unseen mental agencies will finally be shocked into another
6 extreme mortal mood, — into human indignation; for
one extreme follows another.

Revelation xii. 15, 16. And the serpent cast out of his
9 mouth water as a flood, after the woman, that he might
cause her to be carried away of the flood. And the earth
helped the woman, and the earth opened her mouth, and
12 swallowed up the flood which the dragon cast out of his
mouth.

Millions of unprejudiced minds — simple seekers for
15 Truth, weary wanderers, athirst in the desert — are waiting and watching for rest and drink. Give them a cup of
cold water in Christ's name, and never fear the conse-
18 quences. What if the old dragon should send forth a new
flood to drown the Christ-idea? He can neither drown
your voice with its roar, nor again sink the world into the
21 deep waters of chaos and old night. In this age the earth
will help the woman; the spiritual idea will be understood.
Those ready for the blessing you impart will give thanks.
24 The waters will be pacified, and Christ will command the
wave.

When God heals the sick or the sinning, they should
27 know the great benefit which Mind has wrought. They
should also know the great delusion of mortal mind, when
it makes them sick or sinful. Many are willing to open

the eyes of the people to the power of good resident in
divine Mind, but they are not so willing to point out the
evil in human thought, and expose evil's hidden mental
ways of accomplishing iniquity.

Why this backwardness, since exposure is necessary to
ensure the avoidance of the evil? Because people like
you better when you tell them their virtues than when you
tell them their vices. It requires the spirit of our blessed
Master to tell a man his faults, and so risk human dis-
pleasure for the sake of doing right and benefiting our
race. Who is telling mankind of the foe in ambush? Is
the informer one who sees the foe? If so, listen and be
wise. Escape from evil, and designate those as unfaithful
stewards who have seen the danger and yet have given
no warning.

At all times and under all circumstances, overcome evil
with good. Know thyself, and God will supply the wisdom
and the occasion for a victory over evil. Clad in the
panoply of Love, human hatred cannot reach you. The
cement of a higher humanity will unite all interests in the
one divinity.

HYMNS

By Rev. Mary Baker Eddy

1   [Set to the Church Chimes and Sung on This Occasion]

LAYING THE CORNER-STONE

3   *Laus Deo*, it is done!
    Rolled away from loving heart
        Is a stone.
6   Joyous, risen, we depart
        Having one.

    Laus Deo, — on this rock
9   (Heaven chiselled squarely good)
        Stands His church, —
    God is Love, and understood
12   By His flock.

    Laus Deo, night starlit
    Slumbers not in God's embrace;
15   Then, O man!
    Like this stone, be in thy place;
        Stand, not sit.

18   Cold, silent, stately stone,
    Dirge and song and shoutings low,
        In thy heart
21   Dwell serene, — and sorrow? No,
        It has none,
        Laus Deo!

"FEED MY SHEEP"   1

Shepherd, show me how to go
  O'er the hillside steep,
How to gather, how to sow, —   3
  How to feed Thy sheep;
I will listen for Thy voice,   6
  Lest my footsteps stray;
I will follow and rejoice
  All the rugged way.   9

Thou wilt bind the stubborn will,
  Wound the callous breast,
Make self-righteousness be still,   12
  Break earth's stupid rest.
Strangers on a barren shore,
  Lab'ring long and lone —   15
We would enter by the door,
  And Thou know'st Thine own.

So, when day grows dark and cold,   18
  Tear or triumph harms,
Lead Thy lambkins to the fold,
  Take them in Thine arms;   21
Feed the hungry, heal the heart,
  Till the morning's beam;
White as wool, ere they depart —   24
  Shepherd, wash them clean.

CHRIST MY REFUGE

O'er waiting harpstrings of the mind
        There sweeps a strain,
Low, sad, and sweet, whose measures bind
        The power of pain.

And wake a white-winged angel throng
        Of thoughts, illumed
By faith, and breathed in raptured song,
        With love perfumed.

Then his unveiled, sweet mercies show
        Life's burdens light.
I kiss the cross, and wake to know
        A world more bright.

And o'er earth's troubled, angry sea
        I see Christ walk,
And come to me, and tenderly,
        Divinely talk.

Thus Truth engrounds me on the rock,
        Upon Life's shore;
'Gainst which the winds and waves can shock,
        Oh, nevermore!

From tired joy and grief afar,
        And nearer Thee, —
Father, where Thine own children are,
        I love to be.

My prayer, some daily good to do 1
    To Thine, for Thee;
An offering pure of Love, whereto 3
    God leadeth me.

NOTE

By Rev. Mary Baker Eddy

1 The land whereon stands The First Church of Christ, Scientist, in Boston, was first purchased by the church 3 and society. Owing to a heavy loss, they were unable to pay the mortgage; therefore I paid it, and through trustees gave back the land to the church.

6 In 1892 I had to recover the land from the trustees, reorganize the church, and reobtain its charter — not, however, through the State Commissioner, who refused to 9 grant it, but by means of a statute of the State, and through Directors regive the land to the church. In 1895 I reconstructed my original system of ministry and church government. 12 Thus committed to the providence of God, the prosperity of this church is unsurpassed.

From first to last The Mother Church seemed type and 15 shadow of the warfare between the flesh and Spirit, even that shadow whose substance is the divine Spirit, imperatively propelling the greatest moral, physical, civil, 18 and religious reform ever known on earth. In the words of the prophet: "The shadow of a great rock in a weary land."

21 This church was dedicated on January 6, anciently one of the many dates selected and observed in the East as the day of the birth and baptism of our master Metaphysician, 24 Jesus of Nazareth.

Christian Scientists, their children and grandchildren 1
to the latest generations, inevitably love one another with
that love wherewith Christ loveth us; a love unselfish, 3
unambitious, impartial, universal, — that loves only because it *is* Love. Moreover, they love their enemies, even
those that hate them. This we all must do to be Christian 6
Scientists in spirit and in truth. I long, and live, to see
this love demonstrated. I am seeking and praying for it
to inhabit my own heart and to be made manifest in my 9
life. Who will unite with me in this pure purpose, and
faithfully struggle till it be accomplished? Let this be our
Christian endeavor society, which Christ organizes and 12
blesses.

While we entertain due respect and fellowship for what
is good and doing good in all denominations of religion, 15
and shun whatever would isolate us from a true sense of
goodness in others, we cannot serve mammon.

Christian Scientists are really united to only that which 18
is Christlike, but they are not indifferent to the welfare of
any one. To perpetuate a cold distance between our denomination and other sects, and close the door on church 21
or individuals — however much this is done to us — is
not Christian Science. Go not into the way of the un-
christly, but wheresoever you recognize a clear expression 24
of God's likeness, there abide in confidence and hope.

Our unity with churches of other denominations must
rest on the spirit of Christ calling us together. It cannot 27
come from any other source. Popularity, self-aggrandize-
ment, aught that can darken in any degree our spirituality,
must be set aside. Only what feeds and fills the sentiment 30

1 with unworldliness, can give peace and good will towards
men.

3   All Christian churches have one bond of unity, one
nucleus or point of convergence, one prayer, — the Lord's
Prayer. It is matter for rejoicing that we unite in love,
6 and in this sacred petition with every praying assembly
on earth, — "Thy kingdom come. Thy will be done in
earth, as it is in heaven."

9   If the lives of Christian Scientists attest their fidelity
to Truth, I predict that in the twentieth century every
Christian church in our land, and a few in far-off lands,
12 will approximate the understanding of Christian Science
sufficiently to heal the sick in his name. Christ will give
to Christianity his new name, and Christendom will be
15 classified as Christian Scientists.

    When the doctrinal barriers between the churches are
broken, and the bonds of peace are cemented by spiritual
18 understanding and Love, there will be unity of spirit, and
the healing power of Christ will prevail. Then shall Zion
have put on her most beautiful garments, and her waste
21 places budded and blossomed as the rose.

CLIPPINGS FROM NEWSPAPERS

[*Daily Inter-Ocean*, Chicago, December 31, 1894]   1

MARY BAKER EDDY

COMPLETION OF THE FIRST CHURCH OF CHRIST, SCIENTIST, BOSTON   3
— "OUR PRAYER IN STONE" — DESCRIPTION OF THE MOST
UNIQUE STRUCTURE IN ANY CITY — A BEAUTIFUL TEMPLE
AND ITS FURNISHINGS — MRS. EDDY'S WORK AND HER IN-   6
FLUENCE

Boston, Mass., December 28. — *Special Correspond-*
ence. — The "great awakening" of the time of Jonathan   9
Edwards has been paralleled during the last decade by a
wave of idealism that has swept over the country, mani-
festing itself under several different aspects and under   12
various names, but each having the common identity of
spiritual demand. This movement, under the guise of
Christian Science, and ingenuously calling out a closer   15
inquiry into Oriental philosophy, prefigures itself to us
as one of the most potent factors in the social evolution
of the last quarter of the nineteenth century. History   18
shows the curious fact that the closing years of every century are years of more intense life, manifested in unrest
or in aspiration, and scholars of special research, like   21
Prof. Max Muller, assert that the end of a cycle, as is the
latter part of the present century, is marked by peculiar
intimations of man's immortal life.   24

1   The completion of the first Christian Science church erected in Boston strikes a keynote of definite attention.

3 This church is in the fashionable Back Bay, between Commonwealth and Huntington Avenues. It is one of the most beautiful, and is certainly the most unique struc-
6 ture in any city. The First Church of Christ, Scientist, as it is officially called, is termed by its Founder, "Our prayer in stone." It is located at the intersection of Nor-
9 way and Falmouth Streets, on a triangular plot of ground, the design a Romanesque tower with a circular front and an octagonal form, accented by stone porticos and turreted
12 corners. On the front is a marble tablet, with the following inscription carved in bold relief: —

"The First Church of Christ, Scientist, erected Anno
15 Domini 1894. A testimonial to our beloved teacher, the Rev. Mary Baker Eddy, Discoverer and Founder of Christian Science; author of "Science and Health
18 with Key to the Scriptures;" president of the Massachusetts Metaphysical College, and the first pastor of this denomination."

21   THE CHURCH EDIFICE

The church is built of Concord granite in light gray, with trimmings of the pink granite of New Hampshire,
24 Mrs. Eddy's native State. The architecture is Romanesque throughout. The tower is one hundred and twenty feet in height and twenty-one and one half feet square. The en-
27 trances are of marble, with doors of antique oak richly carved. The windows of stained glass are very rich in

pictorial effect. The lighting and cooling of the church — 1
for cooling is a recognized feature as well as heating —
are done by electricity, and the heat generated by two 3
large boilers in the basement is distributed by the four
systems with motor electric power. The partitions are
of iron; the floors of marble in mosaic work, and the 6
edifice is therefore as literally fire-proof as is conceivable.
The principal features are the auditorium, seating eleven
hundred people and capable of holding fifteen hundred; 9
the "Mother's Room," designed for the exclusive use of
Mrs. Eddy; the "directors' room," and the vestry. The
girders are all of iron, the roof is of terra cotta tiles, the 12
galleries are in plaster relief, the window frames are of
iron, coated with plaster; the staircases are of iron, with
marble stairs of rose pink, and marble approaches. 15

The vestibule is a fitting entrance to this magnificent
temple. In the ceiling is a sunburst with a seven-pointed
star, which illuminates it. From this are the entrances 18
leading to the auditorium, the "Mother's Room," and
the directors' room.

The auditorium is seated with pews of curly birch, up- 21
holstered in old rose plush. The floor is in white Italian
mosaic, with frieze of the old rose, and the wainscoting
repeats the same tints. The base and cap are of pink 24
Tennessee marble. On the walls are bracketed oxidized
silver lamps of Roman design, and there are frequent
illuminated texts from the Bible and from Mrs. Eddy's 27
"Science and Health with Key to the Scriptures" im-
panelled. A sunburst in the centre of the ceiling takes
the place of chandeliers. There is a disc of cut glass in 30

decorative designs, covering one hundred and forty-four
electric lights in the form of a star, which is twenty-one
inches from point to point, the centre being of pure white
light, and each ray under prisms which reflect the rainbow
tints. The galleries are richly panelled in relief work.
The organ and choir gallery is spacious and rich beyond
the power of words to depict. The platform — corresponding to the chancel of an Episcopal church — is a
mosaic work, with richly carved seats following the sweep
of its curve, with a lamp stand of the Renaissance period
on either end, bearing six richly wrought oxidized silver
lamps, eight feet in height. The great organ comes from
Detroit. It is one of vast compass, with Æolian attachment, and cost eleven thousand dollars. It is the gift of
a single individual — a votive offering of gratitude for the
healing of the wife of the donor.

The chime of bells includes fifteen, of fine range and
perfect tone.

THE "MOTHER'S ROOM"

The "Mother's Room" is approached by an entrance of
Italian marble, and over the door, in large golden letters on
a marble tablet, is the word "Love." In this room the
mosaic marble floor of white has a Romanesque border and
is decorated with sprays of fig leaves bearing fruit. The
room is toned in pale green with relief in old rose. The
mantel is of onyx and gold. Before the great bay window
hangs an Athenian lamp over two hundred years old,
which will be kept always burning day and night.[1] Lead-

[1] At Mrs. Eddy's request the lamp was not kept burning.

ing off the "Mother's Room" are toilet apartments, with ₁
full-length French mirrors and every convenience.

The directors' room is very beautiful in marble ap- ₃
proaches and rich carving, and off this is a vault for the
safe preservation of papers.

The vestry seats eight hundred people, and opening from ₆
it are three large class-rooms and the pastor's study.

The windows are a remarkable feature of this temple.
There are no "memorial" windows; the entire church is a ₉
testimonial, not a memorial — a point that the members
strongly insist upon.

In the auditorium are two rose windows — one repre- ₁₂
senting the heavenly city which "cometh down from God
out of heaven," with six small windows beneath, emblematic of the six water-pots referred to in John ii. 6. The ₁₅
other rose window represents the raising of the daughter
of Jairus. Beneath are two small windows bearing palms
of victory, and others with lamps, typical of Science and ₁₈
Health.

Another great window tells its pictorial story of the four
Marys — the mother of Jesus, Mary anointing the head of ₂₁
Jesus, Mary washing the feet of Jesus, Mary at the resur-
rection; and the woman spoken of in the Apocalypse,
chapter 12, God-crowned.
                                                            ₂₄

One more window in the auditorium represents the
raising of Lazarus.

In the gallery are windows representing John on the ₂₇
Isle of Patmos, and others of pictorial significance. In
the "Mother's Room" the windows are of still more unique
interest. A large bay window, composed of three separate ₃₀

1 panels, is designed to be wholly typical of the work of Mrs.
Eddy. The central panel represents her in solitude and
3 meditation, searching the Scriptures by the light of a single
candle, while the star of Bethlehem shines down from above.
Above this is a panel containing the Christian Science seal,
6 and other panels are decorated with emblematic designs,
with the legends, "Heal the Sick," "Raise the Dead,"
"Cleanse the Lepers," and "Cast out Demons."
9   The cross and the crown and the star are presented in
appropriate decorative effect. The cost of this church is
two hundred and twenty-one thousand dollars, exclusive
12 of the land — a gift from Mrs. Eddy — which is valued
at some forty thousand dollars.

THE ORDER OF SERVICE

15   The order of service in the Christian Science Church
does not differ widely from that of any other sect, save that
its service includes the use of Mrs. Eddy's book, entitled
18 "Science and Health with Key to the Scriptures," in perhaps equal measure to its use of the Bible. The reading
is from the two alternately; the singing is from a compila-
21 tion called the "Christian Science Hymnal," but its songs
are for the most part those devotional hymns from Herbert,
Faber, Robertson, Wesley, Bowring, and other recog-
24 nized devotional poets, with selections from Whittier and
Lowell, as are found in the hymn-books of the Unitarian
churches. For the past year or two Judge Hanna, for-
27 merly of Chicago, has filled the office of pastor to the
church in this city, which held its meetings in Chickering

Hall, and later in Copley Hall, in the new Grundmann 1
Studio Building on Copley Square. Preceding Judge
Hanna were Rev. D. A. Easton and Rev. L. P. Norcross, 3
both of whom had formerly been Congregational clergymen. The organizer and first pastor of the church here
was Mrs. Eddy herself, of whose work I shall venture to 6
speak, a little later, in this article.

Last Sunday I gave myself the pleasure of attending the
service held in Copley Hall. The spacious apartment was 9
thronged with a congregation whose remarkable earnestness impressed the observer. There was no straggling
of late-comers. Before the appointed hour every seat in the 12
hall was filled and a large number of chairs pressed into
service for the overflowing throng. The music was spirited,
and the selections from the Bible and from Science and 15
Health were finely read by Judge Hanna. Then came his
sermon, which dealt directly with the command of Christ
to "heal the sick, raise the dead, cleanse the lepers, cast 18
out demons." In his admirable discourse Judge Hanna
said that while all these injunctions could, under certain
conditions, be interpreted and fulfilled literally, the 21
special lesson was to be taken spiritually — to cleanse the
leprosy of sin, to cast out the demons of evil thought.
The discourse was able, and helpful in its suggestive 24
interpretation.

THE CHURCH MEMBERS

Later I was told that almost the entire congregation was 27
composed of persons who had either been themselves, or

1 had seen members of their own families, healed by Christian Science treatment; and I was further told that once
3 when a Boston clergyman remonstrated with Judge Hanna
for enticing a separate congregation rather than offering
their strength to unite with churches already established —
6 I was told he replied that the Christian Science Church did
not recruit itself from other churches, but from the graveyards! The church numbers now four thousand members;
9 but this estimate, as I understand, is not limited to the
Boston adherents, but includes those all over the country.
The ceremonial of uniting is to sign a brief "confession of
12 faith," written by Mrs. Eddy, and to unite in communion,
which is not celebrated by outward symbols of bread and
wine, but by uniting in silent prayer.

15   The "confession of faith" includes the declaration that
the Scriptures are the guide to eternal Life; that there is a
Supreme Being, and His Son, and the Holy Ghost, and
18 that man is made in His image. It affirms the atonement;
it recognizes Jesus as the teacher and guide to salvation;
the forgiveness of sin by God, and affirms the power of
21 Truth over error, and the need of living faith at the
moment to realize the possibilities of the divine Life.
The entire membership of Christian Scientists throughout
24 the world now exceeds two hundred thousand people. The
church in Boston was organized by Mrs. Eddy, and the
first meeting held on April 12, 1879. It opened with
27 twenty-six members, and within fifteen years it has grown
to its present impressive proportions, and has now its own
magnificent church building, costing over two hundred
30 thousand dollars, and entirely paid for when its consecra-

tion service on January 6 shall be celebrated. This is certainly a very remarkable retrospect.

Rev. Mary Baker Eddy, the Founder of this denomination and Discoverer of Christian Science, as they term her work in affirming the present application of the principles asserted by Jesus, is a most interesting personality. At the risk of colloquialism, I am tempted to "begin at the beginning" of my own knowledge of Mrs. Eddy, and take, as the point of departure, my first meeting with her and the subsequent development of some degree of familiarity with the work of her life which that meeting inaugurated for me.

MRS. EDDY

It was during some year in the early '80's that I became aware — from that close contact with public feeling resulting from editorial work in daily journalism — that the Boston atmosphere was largely thrilled and pervaded by a new and increasing interest in the dominance of mind over matter, and that the central figure in all this agitation was Mrs. Eddy. To a note which I wrote her, begging the favor of an interview for press use, she most kindly replied, naming an evening on which she would receive me. At the hour named I rang the bell at a spacious house on Columbus Avenue, and I was hardly more than seated before Mrs. Eddy entered the room. She impressed me as singularly graceful and winning in bearing and manner, and with great claim to personal beauty. Her figure was tall, slender, and as flexible in movement as that of a Del-

sarte disciple; her face, framed in dark hair and lighted
by luminous blue eyes, had the transparency and rose-flush
of tint so often seen in New England, and she was magnetic,
earnest, impassioned. No photographs can do the least
justice to Mrs. Eddy, as her beautiful complexion and
changeful expression cannot thus be reproduced. At once
one would perceive that she had the temperament to domi-
nate, to lead, to control, not by any crude self-assertion, but
a spiritual animus. Of course such a personality, with the
wonderful tumult in the air that her large and enthusiastic
following excited, fascinated the imagination. What had
she originated? I mentally questioned this modern St.
Catherine, who was dominating her followers like any ab-
bess of old. She told me the story of her life, so far as outward events may translate those inner experiences which
alone are significant.

Mary Baker was the daughter of Mark and Abigail
(Ambrose) Baker, and was born in Concord, N. H., some-
where in the early decade of 1820–'30. At the time I met
her she must have been some sixty years of age, yet she had
the coloring and the elastic bearing of a woman of thirty,
and this, she told me, was due to the principles of Christian Science. On her father's side Mrs. Eddy came from
Scotch and English ancestry, and Hannah More was a
relative of her grandmother. Deacon Ambrose, her mater-
nal grandfather, was known as a "godly man," and her
mother was a religious enthusiast, a saintly and consecrated
character. One of her brothers, Albert Baker, graduated
at Dartmouth and achieved eminence as a lawyer.

MRS. EDDY AS A CHILD   1

As a child Mary Baker saw visions and dreamed dreams.
When eight years of age she began, like Jeanne d'Arc, to   3
hear "voices," and for a year she heard her name called
distinctly, and would often run to her mother questioning
if she were wanted. One night the mother related to her   6
the story of Samuel, and bade her, if she heard the voice
again to reply as he did: "Speak, Lord, for Thy servant
heareth." The call came, but the little maid was afraid   9
and did not reply. This caused her tears of remorse and
she prayed for forgiveness, and promised to reply if the call
came again. It came, and she answered as her mother had   12
bidden her, and after that it ceased.

These experiences, of which Catholic biographies are
full, and which history not infrequently emphasizes, cer-   15
tainly offer food for meditation. Theodore Parker related
that when he was a lad, at work in a field one day on his
father's farm at Lexington, an old man with a snowy beard   18
suddenly appeared at his side, and walked with him as he
worked, giving him high counsel and serious thought. All
inquiry in the neighborhood as to whence the stranger   21
came or whither he went was fruitless; no one else had
seen him, and Mr. Parker always believed, so a friend has
told me, that his visitor was a spiritual form from another   24
world. It is certainly true that many and many persons,
whose life has been destined to more than ordinary achievement, have had experiences of voices or visions in their   27
early youth.

1 At an early age Miss Baker was married to Colonel Glover, of Charleston, S. C., who lived only a year. She 3 returned to her father's home — in 1844 — and from that time until 1866 no special record is to be made.

In 1866, while living in Lynn, Mass., Mrs. Eddy 6 met with a severe accident, and her case was pronounced hopeless by the physicians. There came a Sunday morning when her pastor came to bid her good-9 by before proceeding to his morning service, as there was no probability that she would be alive at its close. During this time she suddenly became aware of a divine illumina-12 tion and ministration. She requested those with her to withdraw, and reluctantly they did so, believing her delirious. Soon, to their bewilderment and fright, she walked 15 into the adjoining room, "and they thought I had died, and that it was my apparition," she said.

THE PRINCIPLE OF DIVINE HEALING

18 From that hour dated her conviction of the Principle of divine healing, and that it is as true to-day as it was in the days when Jesus of Nazareth walked the earth. "I felt 21 that the divine Spirit had wrought a miracle," she said, in reference to this experience. "How, I could not tell, but later I found it to be in perfect scientific accord with the 24 divine law." From 1866–'69 Mrs. Eddy withdrew from the world to meditate, to pray, to search the Scriptures.

"During this time," she said, in reply to my questions, 27 "the Bible was my only textbook. It answered my questions as to the process by which I was restored to health;

it came to me with a new meaning, and suddenly I appre- 1
hended the spiritual meaning of the teaching of Jesus and
the Principle and the law involved in spiritual Science 3
and metaphysical healing — in a word — Christian
Science."

Mrs. Eddy came to perceive that Christ's healing was not 6
miraculous, but was simply a natural fulfilment of divine
law — a law as operative in the world to-day as it was
nineteen hundred years ago. "Divine Science is begotten 9
of spirituality," she says, "since only the 'pure in heart'
can see God."

In writing of this experience, Mrs. Eddy has said: — 12
"I had learned that thought must be spiritualized in
order to apprehend Spirit. It must become honest, unselfish, and pure, in order to have the least understanding 15
of God in divine Science. The first must become last.
Our reliance upon material things must be transferred to
a perception of and dependence on spiritual things. For 18
Spirit to be supreme in demonstration, it must be supreme
in our affections, and we must be clad with divine power.
I had learned that Mind reconstructed the body, and that 21
nothing else could. All Science is a revelation."

Through homœopathy, too, Mrs. Eddy became convinced of the Principle of Mind-healing, discovering that 24
the more attenuated the drug, the more potent was its
effects.

In 1877 Mrs. Glover married Dr. Asa Gilbert Eddy, of 27
Londonderry, Vermont, a physician who had come into
sympathy with her own views, and who was the first to
place "Christian Scientist" on the sign at his door. Dr. 30

1 Eddy died in 1882, a year after her founding of the Metaphysical College in Boston, in which he taught.

3   The work in the Metaphysical College lasted nine years,
and it was closed (in 1889) in the very zenith of its prosperity, as Mrs. Eddy felt it essential to the deeper founda-
6 tion of her religious work to retire from active contact with
the world. To this College came hundreds and hundreds
of students, from Europe as well as this country. I was
9 present at the class lectures now and then, by Mrs. Eddy's
kind invitation, and such earnestness of attention as was
given to her morning talks by the men and women present
12 I never saw equalled.

MRS. EDDY'S PERSONALITY

On the evening that I first met Mrs. Eddy by her hos-
15 pitable courtesy, I went to her peculiarly fatigued. I came
away in a state of exhilaration and energy that made me
feel I could have walked any conceivable distance. I have
18 met Mrs. Eddy many times since then, and always with
this experience repeated.

Several years ago Mrs. Eddy removed from Columbus
21 to Commonwealth Avenue, where, just beyond Massachusetts Avenue, at the entrance to the Back Bay Park,
she bought one of the most beautiful residences in Boston.
24 The interior is one of the utmost taste and luxury, and the
house is now occupied by Judge and Mrs. Hanna, who are
the editors of *The Christian Science Journal*, a monthly
27 publication, and to whose courtesy I am much indebted
for some of the data of this paper. "It is a pleasure to

give any information for *The Inter-Ocean*," remarked 1
Mrs. Hanna, "for it is the great daily that is so fair and so
just in its attitude toward all questions."   3

The increasing demands of the public on Mrs. Eddy
have been, it may be, one factor in her removal to Concord,
N. H., where she has a beautiful residence, called Pleasant 6
View. Her health is excellent, and although her hair is
white, she retains in a great degree her energy and power;
she takes a daily walk and drives in the afternoon. She   9
personally attends to a vast correspondence; superin-
tends the church in Boston, and is engaged on further
writings on Christian Science. In every sense she is the 12
recognized head of the Christian Science Church. At the
same time it is her most earnest aim to eliminate the element of personality from the faith. "On this point, Mrs. 15
Eddy feels very strongly," said a gentleman to me on
Christmas eve, as I sat in the beautiful drawing-room,
where Judge and Mrs. Hanna, Miss Elsie Lincoln, the 18
soprano for the choir of the new church, and one or two
other friends were gathered.

"Mother feels very strongly," he continued, "the danger 21
and the misfortune of a church depending on any one
personality. It is difficult not to centre too closely around
a highly gifted personality."   24

THE FIRST ASSOCIATION

The first Christian Scientist Association was organized
on July 4, 1876, by seven persons, including Mrs. Eddy. 27
In April, 1879, the church was founded with twenty-six

1 members, and its charter obtained the following June.[1]
Mrs. Eddy had preached in other parishes for five years
3 before being ordained in this church, which ceremony
took place in 1881.

The first edition of Mrs. Eddy's book, Science and
6 Health, was issued in 1875. During these succeeding
twenty years it has been greatly revised and enlarged, and
it is now in its ninety-first edition. It consists of fourteen
9 chapters, whose titles are as follows: "Science, Theology,
Medicine," "Physiology," "Footsteps of Truth," "Creation," "Science of Being," "Christian Science and Spirit-
12 ualism," "Marriage," "Animal Magnetism," "Some
Objections Answered," "Prayer," "Atonement and Eu-
charist," "Christian Science Practice," "Teaching Chris-
15 tian Science," "Recapitulation." Key to the Scriptures,
Genesis, Apocalypse, and Glossary.

The Christian Scientists do not accept the belief we call
18 spiritualism. They believe those who have passed the
change of death are in so entirely different a plane of consciousness that between the embodied and disembodied
21 there is no possibility of communication.

They are diametrically opposed to the philosophy of
Karma and of reincarnation, which are the tenets of
24 theosophy. They hold with strict fidelity to what they
believe to be the literal teachings of Christ.

Yet each and all these movements, however they may
27 differ among themselves, are phases of idealism and manifestations of a higher spirituality seeking expression.

It is good that each and all shall prosper, serving those
30 who find in one form of belief or another their best aid

---

[1] Steps were taken to promote the Church of Christ, Scientist, in April, May, and June; formal organization was accomplished and the charter obtained in August, 1879.

and guidance, and that all meet on common ground in the   1
great essentials of love to God and love to man as a signal
proof of the divine origin of humanity which finds no rest   3
until it finds the peace of the Lord in spirituality. They
all teach that one great truth, that

> God's greatness flows around our incompleteness,   6
> Round our restlessness, His rest.
>
> Elizabeth Barrett Browning

I add on the following page a little poem that I con-   9
sider superbly sweet — from my friend, Miss Whiting,
the talented author of "The World Beautiful." — M. B.
Eddy   12

AT THE WINDOW

[Written for the *Traveller*]

The sunset, burning low,   15
    Throws o'er the Charles its flood of golden light.
Dimly, as in a dream, I watch the flow
    Of waves of light.   18

The splendor of the sky
    Repeats its glory in the river's flow;
And sculptured angels, on the gray church tower,   21
    Gaze on the world below.

Dimly, as in a dream,
    I see the hurrying throng before me pass,   24
But 'mid them all I only see *one* face,
    Under the meadow grass.

1   Ah, love! I only know
        How thoughts of you forever cling to me:
3   I wonder how the seasons come and go
        Beyond the sapphire sea?

LILIAN WHITING

6 April 15, 1888

[*Boston Herald*, January 7, 1895]

[Extract]

9   A TEMPLE GIVEN TO GOD — DEDICATION OF THE
     MOTHER CHURCH OF CHRISTIAN SCIENCE

NOVEL METHOD OF ENABLING SIX THOUSAND BELIEVERS TO
12   ATTEND THE EXERCISES — THE SERVICE REPEATED FOUR
     TIMES — SERMON BY REV. MARY BAKER EDDY, FOUNDER OF
     THE DENOMINATION — BEAUTIFUL ROOM WHICH THE CHILDREN
15   BUILT

With simple ceremonies, four times repeated, in the presence of four different congregations, aggregating 18 nearly six thousand persons, the unique and costly edifice erected in Boston at Norway and Falmouth Streets as a home for The First Church of Christ, Scientist, and a 21 testimonial to the Discoverer and Founder of Christian Science, Rev. Mary Baker Eddy, was yesterday dedicated to the worship of God.

The structure came forth from the hands of the artisans
with every stone paid for — with an appeal, not for more
money, but for a cessation of the tide of contributions
which continued to flow in after the full amount needed
was received. From every State in the Union, and from
many lands, the love-offerings of the disciples of Christian
Science came to help erect this beautiful structure, and
more than four thousand of these contributors came to
Boston, from the far-off Pacific coast and the Gulf States
and all the territory that lies between, to view the new-
built temple and to listen to the Message sent them by
the teacher they revere.

From all New England the members of the denomination gathered; New York sent its hundreds, and even
from the distant States came parties of forty and fifty.
The large auditorium, with its capacity for holding from
fourteen hundred to fifteen hundred persons, was hopelessly
incapable of receiving this vast throng, to say nothing of
nearly a thousand local believers. Hence the service was
repeated until all who wished had heard and seen; and
each of the four vast congregations filled the church to
repletion.

At 7:30 a. m. the chimes in the great stone tower, which
rises one hundred and twenty-six feet above the earth,
rung out their message of "On earth peace, good will
toward men."

Old familiar hymns — "All hail the power of Jesus'
name," and others such — were chimed until the hour for
the dedication service had come.

At 9 a. m. the first congregation gathered. Before this

1 service had closed the large vestry room and the spacious
lobbies and the sidewalks around the church were all
3 filled with a waiting multitude. At 10:30 o'clock another
service began, and at noon still another. Then there was
an intermission, and at 3 p. m. the service was repeated
6 for the last time.

There was scarcely even a minor variation in the exercises at any one of these services. At 10:30 a. m., how-
9 ever, the scene was rendered particularly interesting by
the presence of several hundred children in the central
pews. These were the little contributors to the building
12 fund, whose money was devoted to the "Mother's Room,"
a superb apartment intended for the sole use of Mrs. Eddy.
These children are known in the church as the "Busy
15 Bees," and each of them wore a white satin badge with a
golden beehive stamped upon it, and beneath the beehive
the words, "Mother's Room," in gilt letters.

18 The pulpit end of the auditorium was rich with the
adornment of flowers. On the wall of the choir gallery
above the platform, where the organ is to be hereafter
21 placed, a huge seven-pointed star was hung — a star of
lilies resting on palms, with a centre of white immortelles,
upon which in letters of red were the words: "Love-
24 Children's Offering — 1894."

In the choir and the steps of the platform were potted
palms and ferns and Easter lilies. The desk was wreathed
27 with ferns and pure white roses fastened with a broad
ribbon bow. On its right was a large basket of white
carnations resting on a mat of palms, and on its left a vase
30 filled with beautiful pink roses.

Two combined choirs — that of First Church of Christ, 1
Scientist, of New York, and the choir of the home church,
numbering thirty-five singers in all — led the singing, 3
under the direction, respectively, of Mr. Henry Lincoln
Case and Miss Elsie Lincoln.

Judge S. J. Hanna, editor of *The Christian Science* 6
Journal, presided over the exercises. On the platform
with him were Messrs. Ira O. Knapp, Joseph Armstrong,
Stephen A. Chase, and William B. Johnson, who compose 9
the Board of Directors, and Mrs. Henrietta Clark Bemis,
a distinguished elocutionist, and a native of Concord, New
Hampshire.   12

The utmost simplicity marked the exercises. After an
organ voluntary, the hymn, *"Laus Deo*, it is done!"
written by Mrs. Eddy for the corner-stone laying last 15
spring, was sung by the congregation. Selections from the
Scriptures and from "Science and Health with Key to the
Scriptures," were read by Judge Hanna and Dr. Eddy.   18

A few minutes of silent prayer came next, followed by
the recitation of the Lord's Prayer, with its spiritual interpretation as given in the Christian Science textbook.   21

The sermon prepared for the occasion by Mrs. Eddy,
which was looked forward to as the chief feature of the
dedication, was then read by Mrs. Bemis. Mrs. Eddy 24
remained at her home in Concord, N. H., during the day,
because, as heretofore stated in *The Herald*, it is her
custom to discourage among her followers that sort of 27
personal worship which religious teachers so often receive.

Before presenting the sermon, Mrs. Bemis read the following letter from a former pastor of the church: —   30

"To Rev. Mary Baker Eddy

    "*Dear Teacher, Leader, Guide:* — '*Laus Deo,* it is done!'
At last you begin to see the fruition of that you have worked,
toiled, prayed for. The 'prayer in stone' is accomplished.
Across two thousand miles of space, as mortal sense puts
it, I send my hearty congratulations. You are fully occupied, but I thought you would willingly pause for an
instant to receive this brief message of congratulation.
Surely it marks an era in the blessed onward work of
Christian Science. It is a most auspicious hour in your
eventful career. While we all rejoice, yet the mother in
Israel, alone of us all, comprehends its full significance.

                    "Yours lovingly,

                      "LANSON P. NORCROSS"

[*Boston Sunday Globe*, January 6, 1895]

[Extract]

STATELY HOME FOR BELIEVERS IN GOSPEL HEALING —
    A WOMAN OF WEALTH WHO DEVOTES ALL TO HER
        CHURCH WORK

    Christian Science has shown its power over its students,
as they are called, by building a church by voluntary contributions, the first of its kind; a church which will be
dedicated to-day with a quarter of a million dollars ex-
pended and free of debt.

    The money has flowed in from all parts of the United
States and Canada without any special appeal, and it kept
coming until the custodian of funds cried "enough" and
refused to accept any further checks by mail or otherwise.

Men, women, and children lent a helping hand, some   1
giving a mite and some substantial sums. Sacrifices were
made in many an instance which will never be known in   3
this world.

Christian Scientists not only say that they can effect
cures of disease and erect churches, but add that they can   6
get their buildings finished on time, even when the feat
seems impossible to mortal senses. Read the following,
from a publication of the new denomination: —   9

"One of the grandest and most helpful features of this
glorious consummation is this: that one month before the
close of the year every evidence of material sense declared   12
that the church's completion within the year 1894 tran-
scended human possibility. The predictions of workman
and onlooker alike were that it could not be completed   15
before April or May of 1895. Much was the ridicule
heaped upon the hopeful, trustful ones, who declared and
repeatedly asseverated to the contrary. This is indeed,   18
then, a scientific demonstration. It has proved, in most
striking manner, the oft-repeated declarations of our
textbooks, that the evidence of the mortal senses is   21
unreliable."

A week ago Judge Hanna withdrew from the pastorate
of the church, saying he gladly laid down his responsibili-   24
ties to be succeeded by the grandest of ministers — the
Bible and "Science and Health with Key to the Scriptures." This action, it appears, was the result of rules   27
made by Mrs. Eddy. The sermons hereafter will consist
of passages read from the two books by Readers, who will
be elected each year by the congregation.   30

1   A story has been abroad that Judge Hanna was so eloquent and magnetic that he was attracting listeners who
3 came to hear him preach, rather than in search of the truth as taught. Consequently the new rules were formulated. But at Christian Science headquarters this is denied;
6 Mrs. Eddy says the words of the judge speak to the point, and that no such inference is to be drawn therefrom.

   In Mrs. Eddy's personal reminiscences, which are pub-
9 lished under the title of "Retrospection and Introspection," much is told of herself in detail that can only be touched upon in this brief sketch.

12   Aristocratic to the backbone, Mrs. Eddy takes delight in going back to the ancestral tree and in tracing those branches which are identified with good and great names
15 both in Scotland and England.

   Her family came to this country not long before the Revolution. Among the many souvenirs that Mrs. Eddy
18 remembers as belonging to her grandparents was a heavy sword, encased in a brass scabbard, upon which had been inscribed the name of the kinsman upon whom the sword
21 had been bestowed by Sir William Wallace of mighty Scottish fame.

   Mrs. Eddy applied herself, like other girls, to her studies,
24 though perhaps with an unusual zest, delighting in philosophy, logic, and moral science, as well as looking into the ancient languages, Hebrew, Greek, and Latin.

27   Her last marriage was in the spring of 1877, when, at Lynn, Mass., she became the wife of Asa Gilbert Eddy. He was the first organizer of a Christian Science Sunday
30 School, of which he was the superintendent, and later he

attracted the attention of many clergymen of other de-   1
nominations by his able lectures upon Scriptural topics.
He died in 1882.   3

Mrs. Eddy is known to her circle of pupils and admirers
as the editor and publisher of the first official organ of this
sect. It was called the *Journal of Christian Science*, and   6
has had great circulation with the members of this fast-
increasing faith.

In recounting her experiences as the pioneer of Chris-   9
tian Science, she states that she sought knowledge concerning the physical side in this research through the different
schools of allopathy, homœopathy, and so forth, without   12
receiving any real satisfaction. No ancient or modern
philosophy gave her any distinct statement of the Science
of Mind-healing. She claims that no human reason has   15
been equal to the question. And she also defines carefully the difference in the theories between faith-cure and
Christian Science, dwelling particularly upon the terms   18
belief and understanding, which are the key words respectively used in the definitions of these two healing arts.

Besides her Boston home, Mrs. Eddy has a delightful   21
country home one mile from the State House of New
Hampshire's quiet capital, an easy driving distance for
her when she wishes to catch a glimpse of the world. But   24
for the most part she lives very much retired, driving rather
into the country, which is so picturesque all about Concord and its surrounding villages.   27

The big house, so delightfully remodelled and modern-
ized from a primitive homestead that nothing is left ex-
cepting the angles and pitch of the roof, is remarkably   30

1 well placed upon a terrace that slopes behind the buildings, while they themselves are in the midst of green
3 stretches of lawns, dotted with beds of flowering shrubs,
with here and there a fountain or summer-house.

Mrs. Eddy took the writer straight to her beloved "look-
6 out" — a broad piazza on the south side of the second
story of the house, where she can sit in her swinging chair,
revelling in the lights and shades of spring and summer
9 greenness. Or, as just then, in the gorgeous October
coloring of the whole landscape that lies below, across the
farm, which stretches on through an intervale of beautiful
12 meadows and pastures to the woods that skirt the valley
of the little truant river, as it wanders eastward.

It pleased her to point out her own birthplace. Straight
15 as the crow flies, from her piazza, does it lie on the brow
of Bow hill, and then she paused and reminded the reporter
that Congressman Baker from New Hampshire, her cousin,
18 was born and bred in that same neighborhood. The
photograph of Hon. Hoke Smith, another distinguished
relative, adorned the mantel.

21 Then my eye caught her family coat of arms and the
diploma given her by the Society of the Daughters of the
Revolution.

24 The natural and lawful pride that comes with a tincture
of blue and brave blood, is perhaps one of her characteris-
tics, as is many another well-born woman's. She had a
27 long list of worthy ancestors in Colonial and Revolutionary
days, and the McNeils and General Knox figure largely in
her genealogy, as well as the hero who killed the ill-starred
30 Paugus.

This big, sunny room which Mrs. Eddy calls her den — 1
or sometimes "Mother's room," when speaking of her
many followers who consider her their spiritual Leader — 3
has the air of hospitality that marks its hostess herself.
Mrs. Eddy has hung its walls with reproductions of some
of Europe's masterpieces, a few of which had been the 6
gifts of her loving pupils.

Looking down from the windows upon the tree-tops
on the lower terrace, the reporter exclaimed: "You have 9
lived here only four years, and yet from a barren waste
of most unpromising ground has come forth all this
beauty!" 12

"Four years!" she ejaculated; "two and a half, only
two and a half years." Then, touching my sleeve and
pointing, she continued: "Look at those big elms! I had 15
them brought here in warm weather, almost as big as they
are now, and not one died."

Mrs. Eddy talked earnestly of her friendships. . . . 18
She told something of her domestic arrangements, of how
she had long wished to get away from her busy career in
Boston, and return to her native granite hills, there to 21
build a substantial home that should do honor to that
precinct of Concord.

She chose the stubbly old farm on the road from Con- 24
cord, within one mile of the "Eton of America," St. Paul's
School. Once bought, the will of the woman set at work,
and to-day a strikingly well-kept estate is the first impres- 27
sion given to the visitor as he approaches Pleasant View.

She employs a number of men to keep the grounds and
farm in perfect order, and it was pleasing to learn that this 30

1 rich woman is using her money to promote the welfare of
industrious workmen, in whom she takes a vital interest.

3   Mrs. Eddy believes that "the laborer is worthy of his
hire," and, moreover, that he deserves to have a home and
family of his own. Indeed, one of her motives in buying
6 so large an estate was that she might do something for the
toilers, and thus add her influence toward the advancement
of better home life and citizenship.

---

9   [*Boston Transcript*, December 31, 1894]
                              [Extract]

    The growth of Christian Science is properly marked by
12 the erection of a visible house of worship in this city, which
will be dedicated to-morrow. It has cost two hundred
thousand dollars, and no additional sums outside of the
15 subscriptions are asked for. This particular phase of
religious belief has impressed itself upon a large and increasing number of Christian people, who have been
18 tempted to examine its principles, and doubtless have been
comforted and strengthened by them. Any new movement will awaken some sort of interest. There are many
21 who have worn off the novelty and are thoroughly carried
away with the requirements, simple and direct as they are,
of Christian Science. The opposition against it from the
24 so-called orthodox religious bodies keeps up a while, but
after a little skirmishing, finally subsides. No one religious
body holds the whole of truth, and whatever is likely to
27 show even some one side of it will gain followers and live
down any attempted repression.

Christian Science does not strike all as a system of truth. 1
If it did, it would be a prodigy. Neither does the Christian
faith produce the same impressions upon all. Freedom to 3
believe or to dissent is a great privilege in these days. So
when a number of conscientious followers apply themselves
to a matter like Christian Science, they are enjoying that 6
liberty which is their inherent right as human beings, and
though they cannot escape censure, yet they are to be
numbered among the many pioneers who are searching 9
after religious truth. There is really nothing settled.
Every truth is more or less in a state of agitation. The
many who have worked in the mine of knowledge are glad 12
to welcome others who have different methods, and with
them bring different ideas.

It is too early to predict where this movement will go, 15
and how greatly it will affect the well-established methods.
That it has produced a sensation in religious circles, and
called forth the implements of theological warfare, is very 18
well known. While it has done this, it may, on the other
hand, have brought a benefit. Ere this many a new project
in religious belief has stirred up feeling, but as time has 21
gone on, compromises have been welcomed.

The erection of this temple will doubtless help on the
growth of its principles. Pilgrims from everywhere will go 24
there in search of truth, and some may be satisfied and some
will not. Christian Science cannot absorb the world's
thought. It may get the share of attention it deserves, but 27
it can only aspire to take its place alongside other great
demonstrations of religious belief which have done something good for the sake of humanity. 30

1   Wonders will never cease. Here is a church whose
treasurer has to send out word that no sums except those
3 already subscribed can be received! The Christian
Scientists have a faith of the mustard-seed variety.
What a pity some of our practical Christian folk have not a
6 faith approximate to that of these "impractical" Christian
Scientists.

————

[*Jackson Patriot*, Jackson, Mich., January 20, 1895]

9   [Extract]

CHRISTIAN SCIENCE

The erection of a massive temple in Boston by Christian
12 Scientists, at a cost of over two hundred thousand dollars,
love-offerings of the disciples of Mary Baker Eddy, reviver
of the ancient faith and author of the textbook from which,
15 with the New Testament at the foundation, believers
receive light, health, and strength, is evidence of the rapid
growth of the new movement. We call it new. It is not.
18 The name Christian Science alone is new. At the beginning of Christianity it was taught and practised by Jesus
and his disciples. The Master was the great healer. But
21 the wave of materialism and bigotry that swept over the
world for fifteen centuries, covering it with the blackness
of the Dark Ages, nearly obliterated all vital belief in his
24 teachings. The Bible was a sealed book. Recently a
revived belief in what he taught is manifest, and Christian
Science is one result. No new doctrine is proclaimed, but

there is the fresh development of a Principle that was put
into practice by the Founder of Christianity nineteen hundred years ago, though practised in other countries at an
earlier date. "The thing that hath been, it is that which
shall be; and that which is done is that which shall be
done: and there is no new thing under the sun."

The condition which Jesus of Nazareth, on various
occasions during the three years of his ministry on earth,
declared to be essential, in the mind of both healer and
patient, is contained in the one word — *faith*. Can drugs
suddenly cure leprosy? When the ten lepers were cleansed
and one returned to give thanks in Oriental phrase, Jesus
said to him: "Arise, go thy way: thy faith hath made thee
whole." That was Christian Science. In his "Law of
Psychic Phenomena" Hudson says: "That word, more
than any other, expresses the whole law of human felicity
and power in this world, and of salvation in the world to
come. It is that attribute of mind which elevates man
above the level of the brute, and gives dominion over the
physical world. It is the essential element of success in
every field of human endeavor. It constitutes the power
of the human soul. When Jesus of Nazareth proclaimed
its potency from the hilltops of Palestine, he gave to mankind the key to health and heaven, and earned the title
of Saviour of the World." Whittier, grandest of mystic
poets, saw the truth: —

> That healing gift he lends to them
>   Who use it in his name;
> The power that filled his garment's hem
>   Is evermore the same.

1   Again, in a poem entitled "The Master," he wrote: —

     The healing of his seamless dress
3   Is by our beds of pain;
     We touch him in life's throng and press,
          And we are whole again.[1]

6   That Jesus operated in perfect harmony with natural
     law, not in defiance, suppression, or violation of it, we can-
     not doubt. The perfectly natural is the perfectly spiritual.
9   Jesus enunciated and exemplified the Principle; and,
     obviously, the conditions requisite in psychic healing
     to-day are the same as were necessary in apostolic times.
12   We accept the statement of Hudson: "There was no law
     of nature violated or transcended. On the contrary, the
     whole transaction was in perfect obedience to the laws of
15   nature. He understood the law perfectly, as no one before
     him understood it; and in the plenitude of his power he
     applied it where the greatest good could be accomplished."
18   A careful reading of the accounts of his healings, in the
     light of modern science, shows that he observed, in his
     practice of mental therapeutics, the conditions of environ-
21   ment and harmonious influence that are essential to success.
     In the case of Jairus' daughter they are fully set forth.
     He kept the unbelievers away, "put them all out," and
24   permitting only the father and mother, with his closest
     friends and followers, Peter, James, and John, in the
     chamber with him, and having thus the most perfect
27   obtainable environment, he raised the daughter to life.

     [1] NOTE: — About 1868, the author of Science and Health healed
     Mr. Whittier with one visit, at his home in Amesbury, of incipient
30   pulmonary consumption. — M. B. EDDY

"Not in blind caprice of will,   1
Not in cunning sleight of skill,
Not for show of power, was wrought   3
Nature's marvel in thy thought."

In a previous article we have referred to cyclic changes
that came during the last quarter of preceding centuries. 6
Of our remarkable nineteenth century not the least eventful circumstance is the advent of Christian Science.
That it should be the work of a woman is the natural out- 9
come of a period notable for her emancipation from many
of the thraldoms, prejudices, and oppressions of the past.
We do not, therefore, regard it as a mere coincidence that 12
the first edition of Mrs. Eddy's Science and Health should
have been published in 1875. Since then she has revised
it many times, and the ninety-first edition is announced. 15
Her discovery was first called, "The Science of Divine
Metaphysical Healing." Afterward she selected the name
Christian Science. It is based upon what is held to be 18
scientific certainty, namely, — that all causation is of
Mind, every effect has its origin in desire and thought.
The theology — if we may use the word — of Christian 21
Science is contained in the volume entitled "Science and
Health with Key to the Scriptures."

The present Boston congregation was organized 24
April 12, 1879, and has now over four thousand members.
It is regarded as the parent organization, all others being
branches, though each is entirely independent in the 27
management of its own affairs. Truth is the sole recognized
authority. Of actual members of different congregations
there are between one hundred thousand and two hundred 30

1 thousand. One or more organized societies have sprung
up in New York, Chicago, Buffalo, Cleveland, Cincin-
3 nati, Philadelphia, Detroit, Toledo, Milwaukee, Madison,
Scranton, Peoria, Atlanta, Toronto, and nearly every other
centre of population, besides a large and growing number
6 of receivers of the faith among the members of all the
churches and non-church-going people. In some churches
a majority of the members are Christian Scientists, and, as
9 a rule, are the most intelligent.

Space does not admit of an elaborate presentation on the
occasion of the erection of the temple, in Boston, the
12 dedication taking place on the 6th of January, of one of
the most remarkable, helpful, and powerful movements
of the last quarter of the century. Christian Science
15 has brought hope and comfort to many weary souls. It
makes people better and happier. Welding Christianity
and Science, hitherto divorced because dogma and truth
18 could not unite, was a happy inspiration.

"And still we love the evil cause,
And of the just effect complain;
21 We tread upon life's broken laws,
And mourn our self-inflicted pain."

_____

[*The Outlook*, New York, January 19, 1895]

24 A CHRISTIAN SCIENCE CHURCH

A great Christian Science church was dedicated in Boston on Sunday, the 6th inst. It is located at Norway and
27 Falmouth Streets, and is intended to be a testimonial to

the Discoverer and Founder of Christian Science, the 1
Rev. Mary Baker Eddy. The building is fire-proof, and
cost over two hundred thousand dollars. It is entirely 3
paid for, and contributions for its erection came from every
State in the Union, and from many lands. The auditorium
is said to seat between fourteen and fifteen hundred, and 6
was thronged at the four services on the day of dedication.
The sermon, prepared by Mrs. Eddy, was read by Mrs.
Bemis. It rehearsed the significance of the building, and 9
reenunciated the truths which will find emphasis there.
From the description we judge that it is one of the most
beautiful buildings in Boston, and, indeed, in all New 12
England. Whatever may be thought of the peculiar tenets
of the Christian Scientists, and whatever difference of
opinion there may be concerning the organization of such 15
a church, there can be no question but that the adherents
of this church have proved their faith by their works.

[*American Art Journal*, New York, January 26, 1895] 18

"OUR PRAYER IN STONE"

Such is the excellent name given to a new Boston church.
Few people outside its own circles realize how extensive is 21
the belief in Christian Science. There are several sects of
mental healers, but this new edifice on Back Bay, just off
Huntington Avenue, not far from the big Mechanics 24
Building and the proposed site of the new Music Hall,
belongs to the followers of Rev. Mary Baker Glover Eddy,
a lady born of an old New Hampshire family, who, after 27

1 many vicissitudes, found herself in Lynn, Mass., healed by
the power of divine Mind, and thereupon devoted herself
3 to imparting this faith to her fellow-beings. Coming to
Boston about 1880, she began teaching, gathered an
association of students, and organized a church. For
6 several years past she has lived in Concord, N. H., near
her birthplace, owning a beautiful estate called Pleasant
View; but thousands of believers throughout this country
9 have joined The Mother Church in Boston, and have now
erected this edifice at a cost of over two hundred thousand
dollars, every bill being paid.

12   Its appearance is shown in the pictures we are permitted
to publish. In the belfry is a set of tubular chimes. Inside
is a basement room, capable of division into seven excellent
15 class-rooms, by the use of movable partitions. The main
auditorium has wide galleries, and will seat over a thousand
in its exceedingly comfortable pews. Scarcely any wood-
18 work is to be found. The floors are all mosaic, the steps
marble, and the walls stone. It is rather dark, often too
much so for comfortable reading, as all the windows are of
21 colored glass, with pictures symbolic of the tenets of the
organization. In the ceiling is a beautiful sunburst window.
Adjoining the chancel is a pastor's study; but for an
24 indefinite time their prime instructor has ordained that the
only pastor shall be the Bible, with her book, called
"Science and Health with Key to the Scriptures." In the
27 tower is a room devoted to her, and called "Mother's
Room," furnished with all conveniences for living, should
she wish to make it a home by day or night. Therein is
30 a portrait of her in stained glass; and an electric light,

behind an antique lamp, kept perpetually burning [1] in her honor; though she has not yet visited her temple, which was dedicated on New Year's Sunday in a somewhat novel way.

There was no special sentence or prayer of consecration, but continuous services were held from nine to four o'clock, every hour and a half, so long as there were attendants; and some people heard these exercises four times repeated. The printed program was for some reason not followed, certain hymns and psalms being omitted. There was singing by a choir and congregation. The *Pater Noster* was repeated in the way peculiar to Christian Scientists, the congregation repeating one sentence and the leader responding with its parallel interpretation by Mrs. Eddy. Antiphonal paragraphs were read from the book of Revelation and her work respectively. The sermon, prepared by Mrs. Eddy, was well adapted for its purpose, and read by a professional elocutionist, not an adherent of the order, Mrs. Henrietta Clark Bemis, in a clear emphatic style. The solo singer, however, was a Scientist, Miss Elsie Lincoln; and on the platform sat Joseph Armstrong, formerly of Kansas, and now the business manager of the Publishing Society, with the other members of the Christian Science Board of Directors — Ira O. Knapp, Edward P. Bates, Stephen A. Chase, — gentlemen officially connected with the movement. The children of believing families collected the money for the Mother's Room, and seats were especially set apart for them at the second dedicatory service. Before one service was over and the auditors left by the rear doors, the front vestibule and street (despite

---

[1] At Mrs. Eddy's request the lamp was not kept burning.

1 the snowstorm) were crowded with others, waiting for admission.

3 On the next Sunday the new order of service went into operation. There was no address of any sort, no notices, no explanation of Bible or their textbook. Judge 6 Hanna, who was a Colorado lawyer before coming into this work, presided, reading in clear, manly, and intelligent tones, the *Quarterly* Bible Lesson, which happened 9 that day to be on Jesus' miracle of loaves and fishes. Each paragraph he supplemented first with illustrative Scripture parallels, as set down for him, and then by pas- 12 sages selected for him from Mrs. Eddy's book. The place was again crowded, many having remained over a week from among the thousands of adherents who had come 15 to Boston for this auspicious occasion from all parts of the country. The organ, made by Farrand & Votey in Detroit, at a cost of eleven thousand dollars, is the gift of 18 a wealthy Universalist gentleman, but was not ready for the opening. It is to fill the recess behind the spacious platform, and is described as containing pneumatic wind- 21 chests throughout, and having an Æolian attachment. It is of three-manual compass, C. C. C. to C. 4, 61 notes; and pedal compass, C. C. C. to F. 30. The great organ 24 has double open diapason (stopped bass), open diapason, dulciana, viola di gamba, doppel flute, hohl flute, octave, octave quint, superoctave, and trumpet, — 61 pipes each. 27 The swell organ has bourdon, open diapason, salicional, æoline, stopped diapason, gemshorn, flute harmonique, flageolet, cornet — 3 ranks, 183, — cornopean, oboe, vox 30 humana — 61 pipes each. The choir organ, enclosed in

separate swell-box, has geigen principal, dolce, concert 1
flute, quintadena, fugara, flute d'amour, piccolo harmonique, clarinet, — 61 pipes each. The pedal organ has 3
open diapason, bourdon, lieblich gedeckt (from stop 10),
violoncello-wood, — 30 pipes each. Couplers: swell to
great; choir to great; swell to choir; swell to great oc- 6
taves, swell to great sub-octaves; choir to great sub-
octaves; swell octaves; swell to pedal; great to pedal;
choir to pedal. Mechanical accessories: swell tremulant, 9
choir tremulant, bellows signal; wind indicator. Pedal
movements: three affecting great and pedal stops, three
affecting swell and pedal stops; great to pedal reversing 12
pedal; crescendo and full organ pedal; balanced great
and choir pedal; balanced swell pedal.

Beautiful suggestions greet you in every part of this 15
unique church, which is practical as well as poetic, and
justifies the name given by Mrs. Eddy, which stands at
the head of this sketch.   J. H. W. 18

[*Boston Journal*, January 7, 1895]

CHIMES RANG SWEETLY

Much admiration was expressed by all those fortunate 21
enough to listen to the first peal of the chimes in the tower
of The First Church of Christ, Scientist, corner of Falmouth and Norway Streets, dedicated yesterday. The 24
sweet, musical tones attracted quite a throng of people,
who listened with delight.

The chimes were made by the United States Tubular 27

Bell Company, of Methuen, Mass., and are something of a novelty in this country, though for some time well and favorably known in the Old Country, especially in England.

They are a substitution of tubes of drawn brass for the heavy cast bells of old-fashioned chimes. They have the advantage of great economy of space, as well as of cost, a chime of fifteen bells occupying a space not more than five by eight feet.

Where the old-fashioned chimes required a strong man to ring them, these can be rung from an electric keyboard, and even when rung by hand require but little muscular power to manipulate them and call forth all the purity and sweetness of their tones. The quality of tone is something superb, being rich and mellow. The tubes are carefully tuned, so that the harmony is perfect. They have all the beauties of a great cathedral chime, with infinitely less expense.

There is practically no limit to the uses to which these bells may be put. They can be called into requisition in theatres, concert halls, and public buildings, as they range in all sizes, from those described down to little sets of silver bells that might be placed on a small centre table.

[*The Republic*, Washington, D. C., February 2, 1895]   1

[Extract]

CHRISTIAN SCIENCE   3

MARY BAKER EDDY THE "MOTHER" OF THE IDEA — SHE HAS AN
IMMENSE FOLLOWING THROUGHOUT THE UNITED STATES, AND
A CHURCH COSTING $250,000 WAS RECENTLY BUILT IN HER   6
HONOR AT BOSTON

"My faith has the strength to nourish trees as well as
souls," was the remark Rev. Mary Baker Eddy, the   9
"Mother" of Christian Science, made recently as she
pointed to a number of large elms that shade her delightful country home in Concord, N. H. "I had them brought   12
here in warm weather, almost as big as they are now, and
not one died." This is a remarkable statement, but it is
made by a remarkable woman, who has originated a new   15
phase of religious belief, and who numbers over one hundred thousand intelligent people among her devoted
followers.   18

The great hold she has upon this army was demonstrated in a very tangible and material manner recently,
when "The First Church of Christ, Scientist," erected at   21
a cost of two hundred and fifty thousand dollars, was
dedicated in Boston. This handsome edifice was paid
for before it was begun, by the voluntary contributions of   24
Christian Scientists all over the country, and a tablet im-
bedded in its wall declares that it was built as "a testimonial to our beloved teacher, Rev. Mary Baker Eddy,   27

1 Discoverer and Founder of Christian Science, author of
its textbook, 'Science and Health with Key to the Scrip-
3 tures,' president of the Massachusetts Metaphysical College, and the first pastor of this denomination."

There is usually considerable difficulty in securing suffi-
6 cient funds for the building of a new church, but such was
not the experience of Rev. Mary Baker Eddy. Money
came freely from all parts of the United States. Men,
9 women, and children contributed, some giving a pittance,
others donating large sums. When the necessary amount
was raised, the custodian of the funds was compelled to
12 refuse further contributions, in order to stop the continued
inflow of money from enthusiastic Christian Scientists.

Mrs. Eddy says she discovered Christian Science in
15 1866. She studied the Scriptures and the sciences, she
declares, in a search for the great curative Principle. She
investigated allopathy, homœopathy, and electricity, with-
18 out finding a clew; and modern philosophy gave her no
distinct statement of the Science of Mind-healing. After
careful study she became convinced that the curative
21 Principle was the Deity.

_____

[*New York Tribune*, February 7, 1895]

[Extract]

24 Boston has just dedicated the first church of the Christian Scientists, in commemoration of the Founder of that
sect, the Rev. Mary Baker Eddy, drawing together six
27 thousand people to participate in the ceremonies, showing

that belief in that curious creed is not confined to its 1
original apostles and promulgators, but that it has pene-
trated what is called the New England mind to an un- 3
looked-for extent. In inviting the Eastern churches and
the Anglican fold to unity with Rome, the Holy Father
should not overlook the Boston sect of Christian Scientists, 6
which is rather small and new, to be sure, but is undoubt-
edly an interesting faith and may have a future before it,
whatever attitude Rome may assume toward it. 9

[*Journal*, Kansas City, Mo., January 10, 1895]

[Extract]

GROWTH OF A FAITH   12

Attention is directed to the progress which has been
made by what is called Christian Science by the dedication
at Boston of "The First Church of Christ, Scientist." 15
It is a most beautiful structure of gray granite, and its
builders call it their "prayer in stone," which suggests
to recollection the story of the cathedral of Amiens, whose 18
architectural construction and arrangement of statuary
and paintings made it to be called the Bible of that city.
The Frankish church was reared upon the spot where, in 21
pagan times, one bitter winter day, a Roman soldier parted
his mantle with his sword and gave half of the garment to
a naked beggar; and so was memorialized in art and 24
stone what was called the divine spirit of giving, whose un-
believing exemplar afterward became a saint. The Boston
church similarly expresses the faith of those who believe 27

1 in what they term the divine art of healing, which, to their
minds, exists as much to-day as it did when Christ healed
3 the sick.

The first church organization of this faith was founded
fifteen years ago with a membership of only twenty-six,
6 and since then the number of believers has grown with
remarkable rapidity, until now there are societies in every
part of the country. This growth, it is said, proceeds
9 more from the graveyards than from conversions from
other churches, for most of those who embrace the faith
claim to have been rescued from death miraculously under
12 the injunction to "heal the sick, cleanse the lepers, raise
the dead, cast out demons." They hold with strict fidelity
to what they conceive to be the literal teachings of the
15 Bible as expressed in its poetical and highly figurative
language.

Altogether the belief and service are well suited to
18 satisfy a taste for the mystical which, along many lines, has
shown an uncommon development in this country during
the last decade, and which is largely Oriental in its choice.
21 Such a rapid departure from long respected views as is
marked by the dedication of this church, and others of
kindred meaning, may reasonably excite wonder as to
24 how radical is to be this encroachment upon prevailing
faiths, and whether some of the pre-Christian ideas of
the Asiatics are eventually to supplant those in company
27 with which our civilization has developed.

[*Montreal Daily Herald*, Saturday, February 2, 1895]   1

[Extract]

CHRISTIAN SCIENCE   3

SKETCH OF ITS ORIGIN AND GROWTH — THE MONTREAL BRANCH

"If you would found a new faith, go to Boston," has been said by a great American writer. This is no idle 6 word, but a fact borne out by circumstances. Boston can fairly claim to be the hub of the logical universe, and an accurate census of the religious faiths which are to be 9 found there to-day would probably show a greater number of them than even Max O'Rell's famous enumeration of John Bull's creeds.   12

Christian Science, or the Principle of divine healing, is one of those movements which seek to give expression to a higher spirituality. Founded twenty-five years ago, 15 it was still practically unknown a decade since, but to-day it numbers over a quarter of a million of believers, the majority of whom are in the United States, and is rapidly 18 growing. In Canada, also, there is a large number of members. Toronto and Montreal have strong churches, comparatively, while in many towns and villages single 21 believers or little knots of them are to be found.

It was exactly one hundred years from the date of the Declaration of Independence, when on July 4, 1876, the 24 first Christian Scientist Association was organized by seven persons, of whom the foremost was Mrs. Eddy. The church was founded in April, 1879, with twenty-six 27 members, and a charter was obtained two months later.

Mrs. Eddy assumed the pastorship of the church during
its early years, and in 1881 was ordained, being now known
as the Rev. Mary Baker Eddy.

The Massachusetts Metaphysical College was founded
by Mrs. Eddy in 1881, and here she taught the principles
of the faith for nine years. Students came to it in hundreds from all parts of the world, and many are now pastors
or in practice. The college was closed in 1889, as Mrs.
Eddy felt it necessary for the interests of her religious work
to retire from active contact with the world. She now
lives in a beautiful country residence in her native State.

[*The American*, Baltimore, Md., January 14, 1895]

[Extract]

MRS. EDDY'S DISCIPLES

It is not generally known that a Christian Science congregation was organized in this city about a year ago. It
now holds regular services in the parlor of the residence
of the pastor, at 1414 Linden Avenue. The dedication in
Boston last Sunday of the Christian Science church, called
The Mother Church, which cost over two hundred thousand dollars, adds interest to the Baltimore organization.
There are many other church edifices in the United States
owned by Christian Scientists. Christian Science was
founded by Mrs. Mary Baker Eddy. The Baltimore congregation was organized at a meeting held at the present
location on February 27, 1894.

Dr. Hammond, the pastor, came to Baltimore about three years ago to organize this movement. Miss Cross came from Syracuse, N. Y., about eighteen months ago. Both were under the instruction of Mrs. Mary Baker Eddy, the Founder of the movement.

Dr. Hammond says he was converted to Christian Science by being cured by Mrs. Eddy of a physical ailment some twelve years ago, after several doctors had pronounced his case incurable. He says they use no medicines, but rely on Mind for cure, believing that disease comes from evil and sick-producing thoughts, and that, if they can so fill the mind with good thoughts as to leave no room there for the bad, they can work a cure. He distinguishes Christian Science from the faith-cure, and added: "This Christian Science really is a return to the ideas of primitive Christianity. It would take a small book to explain fully all about it, but I may say that the fundamental idea is that God is Mind, and we interpret the Scriptures wholly from the spiritual or metaphysical standpoint. We find in this view of the Bible the power fully developed to heal the sick. It is not faith-cure, but it is an acknowledgment of certain Christian and scientific laws, and to work a cure the practitioner must understand these laws aright. The patient may gain a better understanding than the Church has had in the past. All churches have prayed for the cure of disease, but they have not done so in an intelligent manner, understanding and demonstrating the Christ-healing."

[*The Reporter*, Lebanon, Ind., January 18, 1895]

[Extract]

DISCOVERED CHRISTIAN SCIENCE

REMARKABLE CAREER OF REV. MARY BAKER EDDY, WHO HAS
OVER ONE HUNDRED THOUSAND FOLLOWERS

Rev. Mary Baker Eddy, Discoverer and Founder of
Christian Science, author of its textbook, "Science and
Health with Key to the Scriptures," president of the Massachusetts Metaphysical College, and first pastor of the
Christian Science denomination, is without doubt one of
the most remarkable women in America. She has within a
few years founded a sect that has over one hundred thousand converts, and very recently saw completed in Boston,
as a testimonial to her labors, a handsome fire-proof church
that cost two hundred and fifty thousand dollars and was
paid for by Christian Scientists all over the country.

Mrs. Eddy asserts that in 1866 she became certain that
"all causation was Mind, and every effect a mental phenomenon." Taking her text from the Bible, she endeav-
ored in vain to find the great curative Principle — the Deity
— in philosophy and schools of medicine, and she con-
cluded that the way of salvation demonstrated by Jesus
was the power of Truth over all error, sin, sickness, and
death. Thus originated the divine or spiritual Science of
Mind-healing, which she termed Christian Science. She
has a palatial home in Boston and a country-seat in
Concord, N. H. The Christian Science Church has a

membership of four thousand, and eight hundred of the 1
members are Bostonians.

———

[*N. Y. Commercial Advertiser*, January 9, 1895] 3

The idea that Christian Science has declined in popularity is not borne out by the voluntary contribution of a
quarter of a million dollars for a memorial church for Mrs. 6
Eddy, the inventor of this cure. The money comes from
Christian Science believers exclusively.

———

[*The Post*, Syracuse, New York, February 1, 1895] 9

DO NOT BELIEVE SHE WAS DEIFIED

CHRISTIAN SCIENTISTS OF SYRACUSE SURPRISED AT THE NEWS
ABOUT MRS. MARY BAKER EDDY, FOUNDER OF THE FAITH 12

Christian Scientists in this city, and in fact all over the
country, have been startled and greatly discomfited over
the announcements in New York papers that Mrs. Mary 15
Baker G. Eddy, the acknowledged Christian Science
Leader, has been exalted by various dignitaries of the
faith. . . . 18
It is well known that Mrs. Eddy has resigned herself
completely to the study and foundation of the faith to which
many thousands throughout the United States are now so 21
entirely devoted. By her followers and cobelievers she is
unquestionably looked upon as having a divine mission to

1 fulfil, and as though inspired in her great task by super-
natural power.

3   For the purpose of learning the feeling of Scientists in this
city toward the reported deification of Mrs. Eddy, a *Post*
reporter called upon a few of the leading members of the
6 faith yesterday and had a number of very interesting con-
versations upon the subject.

Mrs. D. W. Copeland of University Avenue was one of
9 the first to be seen. Mrs. Copeland is a very pleasant and
agreeable lady, ready to converse, and evidently very much
absorbed in the work to which she has given so much of
12 her attention. Mrs. Copeland claims to have been healed
a number of years ago by Christian Scientists, after she
had practically been given up by a number of well-known
15 physicians.

"And for the past eleven years," said Mrs. Copeland,
"I have not taken any medicine or drugs of any kind, and
18 yet have been perfectly well."

In regard to Mrs. Eddy, Mrs. Copeland said that she
was the Founder of the faith, but that she had never
21 claimed, nor did she believe that Mrs. Lathrop had, that
Mrs. Eddy had any power other than that which came
from God and through faith in Him and His teachings.

24   "The power of Christ has been dormant in mankind for
ages," added the speaker, "and it was Mrs. Eddy's mission
to revive it. In our labors we take Christ as an example,
27 going about doing good and healing the sick. Christ has
told us to do his work, naming as one great essential that
we have faith in him.

30   "Did you ever hear of Jesus' taking medicine himself, or

giving it to others?" inquired the speaker. "Then why should we worry ourselves about sickness and disease? If we become sick, God will care for us, and will send to us those who have faith, who believe in His unlimited and divine power. Mrs. Eddy was strictly an ardent follower after God. She had faith in Him, and she cured herself of a deathly disease through the mediation of her God. Then she secluded herself from the world for three years and studied and meditated over His divine Word. She delved deep into the Biblical passages, and at the end of the period came from her seclusion one of the greatest Biblical scholars of the age. Her mission was then the mission of a Christian, to do good and heal the sick, and this duty she faithfully performed. She of herself had no power. But God has fulfilled His promises to her and to the world. If you have faith, you can move mountains."

Mrs. Henrietta N. Cole is also a very prominent member of the church. When seen yesterday she emphasized herself as being of the same theory as Mrs. Copeland. Mrs. Cole has made a careful and searching study in the beliefs of Scientists, and is perfectly versed in all their beliefs and doctrines. She stated that man of himself has no power, but that all comes from God. She placed no credit whatever in the reports from New York that Mrs. Eddy has been accredited as having been deified. She referred the reporter to the large volume which Mrs. Eddy had herself written, and said that no more complete and yet concise idea of her belief could be obtained than by a perusal of it.

[*New York Herald*, February 6, 1895]

MRS. EDDY SHOCKED

[By Telegraph to the *Herald*]

Concord, N. H., February 4, 1895. — The article published in the *Herald* on January 29, regarding a statement made by Mrs. Laura Lathrop, pastor of the Christian Science congregation that meets every Sunday in Hodgson Hall, New York, was shown to Mrs. Mary Baker Eddy, the Christian Science "Discoverer," to-day.

Mrs. Eddy preferred to prepare a written answer to the interrogatory, which she did in this letter, addressed to the editor of the *Herald:* —

"A despatch is given me, calling for an interview to answer for myself, 'Am I the second Christ?'

"Even the question shocks me. What I am is for God to declare in His infinite mercy. As it is, I claim nothing more than what I am, the Discoverer and Founder of Christian Science, and the blessing it has been to mankind which eternity enfolds.

"I think Mrs. Lathrop was not understood. If she said aught with intention to be thus understood, it is not what I have taught her, and not at all as I have heard her talk.

"My books and teachings maintain but one conclusion and statement of the Christ and the deification of mortals.

"Christ is individual, and one with God, in the sense of divine Love and its compound divine ideal.

"There was, is, and never can be but one God, one

Christ, one Jesus of Nazareth. Whoever in any age ex- 1
presses most of the spirit of Truth and Love, the Principle
of God's idea, has most of the spirit of Christ, of that Mind 3
which was in Christ Jesus.

"If Christian Scientists find in my writings, teachings,
and example a greater degree of this spirit than in others, 6
they can justly declare it. But to think or speak of me in
any manner as a Christ, is sacrilegious. Such a statement
would not only be false, but the absolute antipode of Chris- 9
tian Science, and would savor more of heathenism than of
my doctrines.

"MARY BAKER EDDY" 12

[*The Globe*, Toronto, Canada, January 12, 1895]

[Extract]

CHRISTIAN SCIENTISTS 15

DEDICATION TO THE FOUNDER OF THE ORDER OF A BEAUTIFUL
CHURCH AT BOSTON — MANY TORONTO SCIENTISTS PRESENT

The Christian Scientists of Toronto, to the number of 18
thirty, took part in the ceremonies at Boston last Sunday
and for the day or two following, by which the members
of that faith all over North America celebrated the dedica- 21
tion of the church constructed in the great New England
capital as a testimonial to the Discoverer and Founder of
Christian Science, Rev. Mary Baker Eddy. 24

The temple is believed to be the most nearly fire-proof
church structure on the continent, the only combustible

material used in its construction being that used in the doors and pews. A striking feature of the church is a beautiful apartment known as the "Mother's Room," which is approached through a superb archway of Italian marble set in the wall. The furnishing of the "Mother's Room" is described as "particularly beautiful, and blends harmoniously with the pale green and gold decoration of the walls. The floor is of mosaic in elegant designs, and two alcoves are separated from the apartment by rich hangings of deep green plush, which in certain lights has a shimmer of silver. The furniture frames are of white mahogany in special designs, elaborately carved, and the upholstery is in white and gold tapestry. A superb mantel of Mexican onyx with gold decoration adorns the south wall, and before the hearth is a large rug composed entirely of skins of the eider-down duck, brought from the Arctic regions. Pictures and bric-a-brac everywhere suggest the tribute of loving friends. One of the two alcoves is a retiring-room and the other a lavatory in which the plumbing is all heavily plated with gold."

[*Evening Monitor*, Concord, N. H., February 27, 1895]

AN ELEGANT SOUVENIR

REV. MARY BAKER EDDY MEMORIALIZED BY A CHRISTIAN SCIENCE CHURCH

Rev. Mary Baker Eddy, Discoverer of Christian Science, has received from the members of The First Church of Christ, Scientist, Boston, an invitation formally to accept

the magnificent new edifice of worship which the church 1
has just erected.

The invitation itself is one of the most chastely elegant 3
memorials ever prepared, and is a scroll of solid gold,
suitably engraved, and encased in a handsome plush
casket with white silk linings. Attached to the scroll is a 6
golden key of the church structure.

The inscription reads thus: —

"*Dear Mother:* — During the year eighteen hundred and 9
ninety-four a church edifice was erected at the intersection
of Falmouth and Norway Streets, in the city of Boston,
by the loving hands of four thousand members. This 12
edifice is built as a testimonial to Truth, as revealed by
divine Love through you to this age. You are hereby
most lovingly invited to visit and formally accept this 15
testimonial on the twentieth day of February, eighteen
hundred and ninety-five, at high noon.

"The First Church of Christ, Scientist, at Boston, Mass. 18
"By Edward P. Bates,
"Caroline S. Bates

"To the Reverend Mary Baker Eddy, 21
"Boston, January 6th, 1895"

[*People and Patriot*, Concord, N. H., February 27, 1895]

MAGNIFICENT TESTIMONIAL 24

Members of The First Church of Christ, Scientist, at
Boston, have forwarded to Mrs. Mary Baker Eddy of

1 this city, the Founder of Christian Science, a testimonial
which is probably one of the most magnificent examples
3 of the goldsmith's art ever wrought in this country. It is
in the form of a gold scroll, twenty-six inches long, nine
inches wide, and an eighth of an inch thick.

6   It bears upon its face the following inscription, cut in
script letters: —

"Dear Mother: — During the year 1894 a church edi-
9 fice was erected at the intersection of Falmouth and Norway Streets, in the city of Boston, by the loving hands of
four thousand members. This edifice is built as a testi-
12 monial to Truth, as revealed by divine Love through you
to this age. You are hereby most lovingly invited to visit
and formally accept this testimonial on the 20th day of
15 February, 1895, at high noon.

"The First Church of Christ, Scientist, at Boston, Mass.
"By EDWARD P. BATES,

18   "CAROLINE S. BATES
"To the Rev. Mary Baker Eddy,
"Boston, January 6, 1895"

21   Attached by a white ribbon to the scroll is a gold key
to the church door.

The testimonial is encased in a white satin-lined box
24 of rich green velvet.

The scroll is on exhibition in the window of J. C.
Derby's jewelry store.

[*The Union Signal*, Chicago]   1

[Extract]

THE NEW WOMAN AND THE NEW CHURCH   3

The dedication, in Boston, of a Christian Science temple costing over two hundred thousand dollars, and for which the money was all paid in so that no debt had to be taken 6 care of on dedication day, is a notable event. While we are not, and never have been, devotees of Christian Science, it becomes us as students of public questions not to ignore 9 a movement which, starting fifteen years ago, has already gained to itself adherents in every part of the civilized world, for it is a significant fact that one cannot take up 12 a daily paper in town or village — to say nothing of cities — without seeing notices of Christian Science meetings, and in most instances they are held at "headquarters." 15

We believe there are two reasons for this remarkable development, which has shown a vitality so unexpected. The first is that a revolt was inevitable from the crass 18 materialism of the cruder science that had taken possession of men's minds, for as a wicked but witty writer has said, "If there were no God, we should be obliged to in- 21 vent one." There is something in the constitution of man that requires the religious sentiment as much as his lungs call for breath; indeed, the breath of his soul is a 24 belief in God.

But when Christian Science arose, the thought of the world's scientific leaders had become materialistically 27 "lopsided," and this condition can never long continue.

1 There must be a righting-up of the mind as surely as of a
ship when under stress of storm it is ready to capsize. The
3 pendulum that has swung to one extreme will surely find
the other. The religious sentiment in women is so strong
that the revolt was headed by them; this was inevitable
6 in the nature of the case. It began in the most intellectual
city of the freest country in the world — that is to say,
it sought the line of least resistance. Boston is emphati-
9 cally the women's paradise, — numerically, socially, indeed every way. Here they have the largest individuality,
the most recognition, the widest outlook. Mrs. Eddy we
12 have never seen; her book has many a time been sent
us by interested friends, and out of respect to them we
have fairly broken our mental teeth over its granitic peb-
15 bles. That we could not understand it might be rather
to the credit of the book than otherwise. On this subject
we have no opinion to pronounce, but simply state the
18 fact.

We do not, therefore, speak of the system it sets forth,
either to praise or blame, but this much is true: the spirit
21 of Christian Science ideas has caused an army of well-meaning people to believe in God and the power of faith, who
did not believe in them before. It has made a myriad of
24 women more thoughtful and devout; it has brought a
hopeful spirit into the homes of unnumbered invalids.
The belief that "thoughts are things," that the invisible
27 is the only real world, that we are here to be trained into
harmony with the laws of God, and that what we are here
determines where we shall be hereafter — all these ideas
30 are Christian.

The chimes on the Christian Science temple in Boston 1
played "All hail the power of Jesus' name," on the morning of the dedication. We did not attend, but we learn 3
that the name of Christ is nowhere spoken with more
reverence than it was during those services, and that he
is set forth as the power of God for righteousness and the 6
express image of God for love.

[*The New Century*, Boston, February, 1895]

ONE POINT OF VIEW — THE NEW WOMAN   9

We all know her — she is simply the woman of the past
with an added grace — a newer charm. Some of her
dearest ones call her "selfish" because she thinks so much 12
of herself she spends her whole time helping others. She
represents the composite beauty, sweetness, and nobility
of all those who scorn self for the sake of love and her 15
handmaiden duty — of all those who seek the brightness
of truth not as the moth to be destroyed thereby, but as
the lark who soars and sings to the great sun. She is of 18
those who have so much to give they want no time to take,
and their name is legion. She is as full of beautiful possibilities as a perfect harp, and she realizes that all the har- 21
monies of the universe are in herself, while her own soul
plays upon magic strings the unwritten anthems of love.
She is the apostle of the true, the beautiful, the good, com- 24
missioned to complete all that the twelve have left undone.
Hers is the mission of missions — the highest of all — to

1 make the body not the prison, but the palace of the soul, with the brain for its great white throne.

3   When she comes like the south wind into the cold haunts of sin and sorrow, her words are smiles and her smiles are the sunlight which heals the stricken soul. Her hand is
6 tender — but steel tempered with holy resolve, and as one whom her love had glorified once said — she is soft and gentle, but you could no more turn her from her
9 course than winter could stop the coming of spring. She has long learned with patience, and to-day she knows many things dear to the soul far better than her teachers.
12 In olden times the Jews claimed to be the conservators of the world's morals — they treated woman as a chattel, and said that because she was created after man, she was
15 created solely for man. Too many still are Jews who never called Abraham "Father," while the Jews themselves have long acknowledged woman as man's proper
18 helpmeet. In those days women had few lawful claims and no one to urge them. True, there were Miriam and Esther, but they sang and sacrificed for their people, not
21 for their sex.

To-day there are ten thousand Esthers, and Miriams by the million, who sing best by singing most for their
24 own sex. They are demanding the right to help make the laws, or at least to help enforce the laws upon which depends the welfare of their husbands, their chil-
27 dren, and themselves. Why should our selfish self longer remain deaf to their cry? The date is no longer B. C. Might no longer makes right, and in this fair land at least
30 fear has ceased to kiss the iron heel of wrong. Why then

should we continue to demand woman's love and woman's help while we recklessly promise as lover and candidate what we never fulfil as husband and office-holder? In our secret heart our better self is shamed and dishonored, and appeals from Philip drunk to Philip sober, but has not yet the moral strength and courage to prosecute the appeal. But the east is rosy, and the sunlight cannot long be delayed. Woman must not and will not be disheartened by a thousand denials or a million of broken pledges. With the assurance of faith she prays, with the certainty of inspiration she works, and with the patience of genius she waits. At last she is becoming "as fair as the morn, as bright as the sun, and as terrible as an army with banners" to those who march under the black flag of oppression and wield the ruthless sword of injustice.

In olden times it was the Amazons who conquered the invincibles, and we must look now to their daughters to overcome our own allied armies of evil and to save us from ourselves. She must and will succeed, for as David sang — "God shall help her, and that right early." When we try to praise her later works it is as if we would pour incense upon the rose. It is the proudest boast of many of us that we are "bound to her by bonds dearer than freedom," and that we live in the reflected royalty which shines from her brow. We rejoice with her that at last we begin to know what John on Patmos meant — "And there appeared a great wonder in heaven, a woman clothed with the sun, and the moon under her feet, and upon her head a crown of twelve stars." She brought to warring men the Prince of Peace, and he, departing, left his scepter

1 not in her hand, but in her soul. "The time of times"
is near when "the new woman" shall subdue the whole
3 earth with the weapons of peace. Then shall wrong be
robbed of her bitterness and ingratitude of her sting,
revenge shall clasp hands with pity, and love shall dwell
6 in the tents of hate; while side by side, equal partners in
all that is worth living for, shall stand the new man with
the new woman.

————————

9   [*The Christian Science Journal*, January, 1895]

[Extract]

THE MOTHER CHURCH

12   The Mother Church edifice — The First Church of
Christ, Scientist, in Boston, is erected. The close of the
year, Anno Domini 1894, witnessed the completion of
15 "our prayer in stone," all predictions and prognostications
to the contrary notwithstanding.

Of the significance of this achievement we shall not
18 undertake to speak in this article. It can be better felt
than expressed. All who are awake thereto have some
measure of understanding of what it means. But only
21 the future will tell the story of its mighty meaning or un-
fold it to the comprehension of mankind. It is enough for
us now to know that all obstacles to its completion have
24 been met and overcome, and that our temple is completed
as God intended it should be.

This achievement is the result of long years of untiring,
27 unselfish, and zealous effort on the part of our beloved
teacher and Leader, the Reverend Mary Baker Eddy,
the Discoverer and Founder of Christian Science, who

nearly thirty years ago began to lay the foundation of
this temple, and whose devotion and consecration to God
and humanity during the intervening years have made
its erection possible.

Those who now, in part, understand her mission, turn
their hearts in gratitude to her for her great work, and
those who do not understand it will, in the fulness of time,
see and acknowledge it. In the measure in which she has
unfolded and demonstrated divine Love, and built up in
human consciousness a better and higher conception of
God as Life, Truth, and Love, — as the divine Principle
of all things which really exist, — and in the degree in
which she has demonstrated the system of healing of Jesus
and the apostles, surely she, as the one chosen of God to
this end, is entitled to the gratitude and love of all who
desire a better and grander humanity, and who believe
it to be possible to establish the kingdom of heaven upon
earth in accordance with the prayer and teachings of
Jesus Christ.

[*Concord Evening Monitor*, March 23, 1895]

TESTIMONIAL AND GIFT

To Rev. Mary Baker Eddy, from The First Church of
Christ, Scientist, in Boston

Rev. Mary Baker Eddy received Friday, from the Christian Science Board of Directors, Boston, a beautiful and
unique testimonial of the appreciation of her labors and
loving generosity in the Cause of their common faith. It
was a facsimile of the corner-stone of the new church of

1 the Christian Scientists, just completed, being of granite, about six inches in each dimension, and contains a solid
3 gold box, upon the cover of which is this inscription: —

"To our Beloved Teacher, the Reverend Mary Baker Eddy, Discoverer and Founder of Christian Science, from
6 her affectionate Students, the Christian Science Board of Directors."

On the under side of the cover are the facsimile sig-
9 natures of the Directors, — Ira O. Knapp, William B. Johnson, Joseph Armstrong, and Stephen A. Chase, with the date, "1895." The beautiful souvenir is en-
12 cased in an elegant plush box.

Accompanying the stone testimonial was the following address from the Board of Directors: —

15   Boston, March 20, 1895

To the Reverend Mary Baker Eddy, our Beloved Teacher and Leader: — We are happy to announce to you
18 the completion of The First Church of Christ, Scientist, in Boston.

In behalf of your loving students and all contributors
21 wherever they may be, we hereby present this church to you as a testimonial of love and gratitude for your labors and loving sacrifice, as the Discoverer and Founder of
24 Christian Science, and the author of its textbook, "Science and Health with Key to the Scriptures."

We therefore respectfully extend to you the invitation
27 to become the permanent pastor of this church, in connection with the Bible and the book alluded to above, which you have already ordained as our pastor. And we

most cordially invite you to be present and take charge 1
of any services that may be held therein. We especially
desire you to be present on the twenty-fourth day of March, 3
eighteen hundred and ninety-five, to accept this offering,
with our humble benediction.

Lovingly yours,   6

IRA O. KNAPP,   JOSEPH ARMSTRONG,
WILLIAM B. JOHNSON,   STEPHEN A. CHASE,

The Christian Science Board of Directors   9

REV. MRS. EDDY'S REPLY

Beloved Directors and Brethren: — For your costly offering, and kind call to the pastorate of "The First Church 12
of Christ, Scientist," in Boston — accept my profound
thanks. But permit me, respectfully, to decline their acceptance, while I fully appreciate your kind intentions. 15
If it will comfort you in the least, make me your *Pastor
Emeritus,* nominally. Through my book, your textbook,
I already speak to you each Sunday. You ask too much 18
when asking me to accept your grand church edifice. I
have more of earth now, than I desire, and less of heaven;
so pardon my refusal of that as a material offering. More 21
effectual than the forum are our states of mind, to bless
mankind. This wish stops not with my pen — God give
you grace. As our church's tall tower detains the sun, 24
so may luminous lines from your lives linger, a legacy to
our race.

MARY BAKER EDDY   27

March 25, 1895

LIST OF LEADING NEWSPAPERS WHOSE ARTICLES
ARE OMITTED

From Canada to New Orleans, and from the Atlantic
to the Pacific ocean, the author has received leading newspapers with uniformly kind and interesting articles on
the dedication of The Mother Church. They were, however, too voluminous for these pages. To those which are
copied she can append only a few of the names of other
prominent newspapers whose articles are reluctantly
omitted.

EASTERN STATES

Advertiser, Calais, Me.
Advertiser, Boston, Mass.
Farmer, Bridgeport, Conn.
Independent, Rockland, Mass.
Kennebec Journal, Augusta, Me.
News, New Haven, Conn.
News, Newport, R. I.
Post, Boston, Mass.
Post, Hartford, Conn.
Republican, Springfield, Mass.
Sentinel, Eastport, Me.
Sun, Attleboro, Mass.

MIDDLE STATES

Advertiser, New York City.
Bulletin, Auburn, N. Y.
Daily, York, Pa.
Evening Reporter, Lebanon, Pa.
Farmer, Bridgeport, N. Y.
Herald, Rochester, N. Y.
Independent, Harrisburg, Pa.
Inquirer, Philadelphia, Pa.

1   *News-Tribune*, Duluth, Minn.
        Pioneer-Press, St. Paul, Minn.
3   *Post-Intelligencer*, Seattle, Wash.
        Salt Lake Herald, Salt Lake City, Utah.
        Sentinel, Indianapolis, Ind.
6   *Sentinel*, Milwaukee, Wis.
        Star, Kansas City, Mo.
        Telegram, Portland, Ore.
9   *Times*, Chicago, Ill.
        Times, Minneapolis, Minn.
        Tribune, Minneapolis, Minn.
12   *Tribune*, Salt Lake City, Utah.

        Free Press, London, Can.

Christian Science
versus
Pantheism

Christian Science

versus

Pantheism

by

Mary Baker Eddy

Discoverer and Founder of Christian Science
and Author of Science and Health with
Key to the Scriptures

Published by the
Trustees under the Will of Mary Baker G. Eddy
Boston, U. S. A.

Authorized Literature of

The First Church of Christ, Scientist

in Boston, Massachusetts

Christian Science versus Pantheism

SUBJECT: *Not Pantheism, but Christian Science*

BELOVED brethren, since last you gathered at the
feast of our Passover, the winter winds have come 6
and gone; the rushing winds of March have shrieked and
hummed their hymns; the frown and smile of April, the
laugh of May, have fled; and the roseate blush of joyous 9
June is here and ours.

In unctuous unison with nature, mortals are hoping and
working, putting off outgrown, wornout, or soiled gar- 12
ments — the pleasures and pains of sensation and the
sackcloth of waiting — for the springtide of Soul. For
what a man seeth he hopeth not for, but hopeth for what 15
he hath not seen, and waiteth patiently the appearing
thereof. The night is far spent, and day is not distant in
the horizon of Truth — even the day when all people 18
shall know and acknowledge one God and one Christianity.

CHRISTIAN SCIENCE NOT PANTHEISM

At this period of enlightenment, a declaration from the pulpit that Christian Science is pantheism is anomalous to those who know whereof they speak — who know that Christian Science *is* Science, and therefore is neither hypothetical nor dogmatical, but demonstrable, and looms above the mists of pantheism higher than Mt. Ararat above the deluge.

ANALYSIS OF ''PANTHEISM''

According to Webster the word "pantheism" is derived from two Greek words meaning "all" and "god." Webster's *derivation* of the English word "pantheism" is most suggestive. His uncapitalized word "god" gives the meaning of pantheism as a human opinion of "gods many," or mind in matter. "The doctrine that the universe, conceived of as a whole, is God; that there is no God but the combined forces and laws which are manifested in the existing universe."

The Standard Dictionary has it that pantheism is the doctrine of the deification of natural causes, conceived as one personified nature, to which the religious sentiment is directed.

Pan is a Greek prefix, but it might stand, in the term pantheism, for the mythological deity of that name; and *theism* for a belief concerning Deity in theology. However, Pan in imagery is preferable to pantheism in theology.

The mythical deity may please the fancy, while pantheism   1
suits not at all the Christian sense of religion. Pan, as a
deity, is supposed to preside over sylvan solitude, and is a   3
horned and hoofed animal, half goat and half man, that
poorly presents the poetical phase of the genii of forests.[1]

My sense of nature's rich glooms is, that loneness lacks   6
but one charm to make it half divine — a friend, with
whom to whisper, "Solitude is sweet." Certain moods
of mind find an indefinable pleasure in stillness, soft,   9
silent as the storm's sudden hush; for nature's stillness
is voiced with a hum of harmony, the gentle murmur of
early morn, the evening's closing vespers, and lyre of bird   12
and brooklet.

> "O sacred solitude! divine retreat!
> Choice of the prudent! envy of the great!   15
> By thy pure stream, or in thy evening shade,
> We court fair wisdom, that celestial maid."

Theism is the belief in the personality and infinite mind   18
of one supreme, holy, self-existent God, who reveals Himself supernaturally to His creation, and whose laws are
not reckoned as science. In religion, it is a belief in one   21
God, or in many gods. It is opposed to atheism and

[1] In Roman mythology (one of my girlhood studies), Pan stood
for "universal nature proceeding from the divine Mind and provi-   24
dence, of which heaven, earth, sea, the eternal fire, are so many members." Pan was the god of shepherds and hunters, leader of the
nymphs, president of the mountains, patron of country life, and guar-   27
dian of flocks and herds. His pipe of seven reeds denotes the celestial
harmony of the seven planets; his shepherd's crook, that care and
providence by which he governs the universe; his spotted skin, the   30
stars; his goat's feet, the solidity of the earth; his man-face, the
celestial world.

1 monotheism, but agrees with certain forms of pantheism
and polytheism. It is the doctrine that the universe owes
3 its origin and continuity to the reason, intellect, and will of
a self-existent divine Being, who possesses all wisdom,
goodness, and power, and is the creator and preserver of
6 man.

A theistic theological belief may agree with physics and
anatomy that reason and will are properly classified as
9 mind, located in the brain; also, that the functions of
these faculties depend on conditions of matter, or brain,
for their proper exercise. But reason and will are human;
12 God is divine. In academics and in religion it is patent
that will is capable of use and of abuse, of right and wrong
action, while God is incapable of evil; that brain is matter,
15 and that there are many so-called minds; that He is the
creator of man, but that man also is a creator, making
two creators; but God is Mind and one.

18 GOD — NOT HUMAN DEVICES — THE PRESERVER
OF MAN

God, Spirit, is indeed the preserver of man. Then, in
21 the words of the Hebrew singer, "Why art thou cast down,
O my soul? and why art thou disquieted within me? hope
thou in God: for I shall yet praise Him, who is the health
24 of my countenance, and my God. . . . Who forgiveth
all thine iniquities; who healeth all thy diseases." This
being the case, what need have we of drugs, hygiene, and
27 medical therapeutics, if these are not man's preservers?
By admitting self-evident affirmations and then contra-

dicting them, monotheism is lost and pantheism is found
in scholastic theology. Can a single quality of God,
Spirit, be discovered in matter? The Scriptures plainly
declare, "The Word was God;" and "all things were
made by Him," — the Word. What, then, can matter
create, or how can it exist?

JESUS' DEFINITION OF EVIL

Did God create evil? or is evil self-existent, and so
possessed of the nature of God, good? Since evil is not
self-made, who or what hath made evil? Our Master
gave the proper answer for all time to this hoary query.
He said of evil: "Ye are of your father, the devil, and the
lusts of your father ye will do. He was a murderer from
the beginning, and abode not in the truth [God], because
there is no truth [reality] in him [evil]. When he speaketh
a lie, he speaketh of his own: for he is a liar, and the father
of it [a lie]."

Jesus' definition of devil (evil) explains evil. It shows
that evil is both liar and lie, a delusion and illusion. Therefore we should neither believe the lie, nor believe that it
hath embodiment or power; in other words, we should
not believe that a lie, nothing, can be something, but deny
it and prove its falsity. After this manner our Master cast
out evil, healed the sick, and saved sinners. Knowing
that evil is a lie, and, as the Scripture declares, brought
sin, sickness, and death into the world, Jesus treated the
lie summarily. He denied it, cast it out of mortal mind,
and thus healed sickness and sin. His treatment of evil

1 and disease, Science will restore and establish, — first,
because it was more effectual than all other means; and,
3 second, because evil and disease will never disappear in
any other way.

Finally, brethren, let us continue to denounce evil as the
6 illusive claim that God is not supreme, and continue to
fight it until it disappears, — but not as one that beateth
the mist, but lifteth his head above it and putteth his foot
9 upon a lie.

EVIL, AS PERSONIFIED BY THE SERPENT

Mosaic theism introduces evil, first, in the form of a
12 talking serpent, contradicting the word of God and thereby
obtaining social prestige, a large following, and changing
the order and harmony of God's creation. But the higher
15 criticism is not satisfied with this theism, and asks, If God
is *infinite* good, what and where is evil? And if Spirit
made all that was made, how can matter be an intelligent
18 creator or coworker with God? Again: Did one Mind,
or two minds, enter into the Scriptural allegory, in the
colloquy between good and evil, God and a serpent? — and
21 if two minds, what becomes of theism in Christianity? For
if God, good, is Mind, and evil also is mind, the Christian
religion has at least two Gods. If Spirit is sovereign, how
24 can matter be force or law; and if God, good, is omnipotent, what power hath evil?

It is plain that elevating evil to the altitude of mind gives
27 it power, and that the belief in more than one spirit, if

Spirit, God, is infinite, breaketh the First Commandment   1
in the Decalogue.

Science shows that a plurality of minds, or intelligent   3
matter, signifies more than one God, and thus prevents the
demonstration that the healing Christ, Truth, gave and
gives in proof of the omnipotence of one divine, infinite   6
Principle.

Does not the theism or belief, that after God, Spirit, had
created all things spiritually, a material creation took   9
place, and God, the preserver of man, declared that man
should die, lose the character and sovereignty of Jehovah,
and hint the gods of paganism?   12

THEISTIC RELIGIONS

We know of but three theistic religions, the Mosaic, the
Christian, and the Mohammedan. Does not each of these   15
religions mystify the absolute oneness and infinity of God,
Spirit?

A close study of the Old and New Testaments in con-   18
nection with the original text indicates, in the third chapter of Genesis, a lapse in the Mosaic religion, wherein
theism seems meaningless, or a vague apology for con-   21
tradictions. It certainly gives to matter and evil reality
and power, intelligence and law, which implies Mind,
Spirit, God; and the logical sequence of this error is idol-   24
atry — other gods.

Again: The hypothesis of mind in matter, or more than
one Mind, lapses into evil dominating good, matter govern-   27
ing Mind, and makes sin, disease, and death inevitable,

despite of Mind, or by the consent of Mind! Next, it
follows that the disarrangement of matter causes a man to
be mentally deranged; and the Babylonian sun god, moon
god, and sin god find expression in sun worship, lunacy,
sin, and mortality.

Does not the belief that Jesus, the man of Galilee, is
God, imply two Gods, one the divine, infinite Person, the
other a human finite personality? Does not the belief
that Mary was the mother of God deny the self-existence
of God? and does not the doctrine that Mohammed is
the only prophet of God infringe the sacredness of one
Christ Jesus?

SCIENTIFIC CHRISTIANITY MEANS ONE GOD

Christianity, as taught and demonstrated in the first
century by our great Master, virtually annulled the so-
called laws of matter, idolatry, pantheism, and polytheism.
Christianity then had one God and one law, namely,
divine Science. It said, "Call no man your father upon
the earth, for one is your Father, which is in heaven."
Speaking of himself, Jesus said, "My Father is greater
than I." Christianity, as he taught and demonstrated it,
must ever rest on the basis of the First Commandment and
love for man.

The doctrines that embrace pantheism, polytheism, and
paganism are admixtures of matter and Spirit, truth and
error, sickness and sin, life and death. They make man
the servant of matter, living by reason of it, suffering because of it, and dying in consequence of it. They con-

stantly reiterate the belief of pantheism, that mind "sleeps
in the mineral, dreams in the animal, and wakes in man."

"Infinite Spirit" means one God and His creation, and
no reality in aught else. The term "spirits" means more
than one Spirit; — in paganism they stand for gods; in
spiritualism they imply men and women; and in Christianity they signify a good Spirit and an evil spirit.

Is there a religion under the sun that hath demonstrated
one God and the four first rules pertaining thereto, namely,
"Thou shalt have no other gods before me;" "Love thy
neighbor as thyself;" "Be ye therefore perfect, even as
your Father which is in heaven is perfect;" "Whosoever
liveth and believeth in me shall never die." (John xi. 26.)

What mortal to-day is wise enough to do himself no
harm, to hinder not the attainment of scientific Christianity? Whoever demonstrates the highest humanity, —
long-suffering, self-surrender, and spiritual endeavor to
bless others, — ought to be aided, not hindered, in his
holy mission. I would kiss the feet of such a messenger,
for to help such a one is to help one's self. The demonstration of Christianity blesses all mankind. It loves one's
neighbor as one's self; it loves its enemies — and this
love benefits its enemies (though they believe it not), and
rewards its possessor; for, "If ye love them which love you,
what reward have ye?"

MAN THE TRUE IMAGE OF GOD

From a material standpoint, the best of people sometimes object to the philosophy of Christian Science, on the

1 ground that it takes away man's personality and makes
man less than man. But what saith the apostle? — even
3 this: "If a man think himself to be something, when he is
nothing, he deceiveth himself." The great Nazarene
Prophet said, "By their fruits ye shall know them:" then,
6 if the effects of Christian Science on the lives of men
be thus judged, we are sure the honest verdict of humanity will attest its uplifting power, and prevail over the
9 opposite notion that Christian Science lessens man's individuality.

The students at the Massachusetts Metaphysical Col-
12 lege, generally, were the average man and woman. But
after graduation, the best students in the class averred
that they were stronger and better than before it. With
15 twelve lessons or less, the present and future of those students had wonderfully broadened and brightened before
them, thus proving the utility of what they had been taught.
18 Christian Scientists heal functional, organic, chronic, and
acute diseases that M.D.'s have failed to heal; and,
better still, they reform desperate cases of intemperance,
21 tobacco using, and immorality, which, we regret to say,
other religious teachers are unable to effect. All this is
accomplished by the grace of God, — the effect of God
24 *understood*. A higher manhood is manifest, and never
lost, in that individual who finds the highest joy, — therefore no pleasure in loathsome habits or in sin, and no
27 necessity for disease and death. Whatever promotes
statuesque being, health, and holiness does not degrade
man's personality. Sin, sickness, appetites, and passions,
30 constitute no part of man, but obscure man. Therefore it

required the divinity of our Master to perceive the real
man, and to cast out the unreal or counterfeit. It caused
St. Paul to write, — "Lie not one to another, seeing that
ye have put off the old man with his deeds; and have put
on the new man, which is renewed in knowledge after
the image of Him that created him."

Was our Master mistaken in judging a cause by its
effects? Shall the opinions, systems, doctrines, and dogmas of men gauge the animus of man? or shall his stature
in Christ, Truth, declare him? Governed by the divine
Principle of his being, man is perfect. When will the
schools allow mortals to turn from clay to Soul for the
model? The Science of being, understood and obeyed,
will demonstrate man to be superior to the best church-
member or moralist on earth, who understands not this
Science. If man is spiritually fallen, it matters not what
he believes; he is not upright, and must regain his native
spiritual stature in order to be in proper shape, as certainly
as the man who falls physically needs to rise again.

Mortals, content with something less than perfection —
the original standard of man — may believe that evil de-
velops good, and that whatever strips off evil's disguise belittles man's personality. But God enables us to know that
evil is not the medium of good, and that good supreme destroys all sense of evil, obliterates the lost image that
mortals are content to call man, and demands man's unfallen spiritual perfectibility.

The grand realism that man is the true image of God,
not fallen or inverted, is demonstrated by Christian Science.
And because Christ's dear demand, "Be ye therefore

1 perfect," is valid, it will be found possible to fulfil it. Then
also will it be learned that good is not educed from evil,
3 but comes from the rejection of evil and its *modus operandi.*
Our scholarly expositor of the Scriptures, Lyman Abbott,
D.D., writes, "God, Spirit, is ever in universal nature."
6 Then, we naturally ask, how can Spirit be constantly passing out of mankind by death — for the universe includes
man?

9   THE GRANDEUR OF CHRISTIANITY

This closing century, and its successors, will make strong
claims on religion, and demand that the inspired Scriptural
12 commands be fulfilled. The altitude of Christianity openeth, high above the so-called laws of matter, a door that no
man can shut; it showeth to all peoples the way of escape
15 from sin, disease, and death; it lifteth the burden of sharp
experience from off the heart of humanity, and so lighteth
the path that he who entereth it may run and not weary,
18 and walk, not wait by the roadside, — yea, pass gently on
without the alterative agonies whereby the way-seeker
gains and points the path.
21   The Science of Christianity is strictly monotheism, —
it has ONE GOD. And this divine infinite Principle,
noumenon and phenomena, is demonstrably the self-
24 existent Life, Truth, Love, substance, Spirit, Mind, which
includes all that the term implies, and is all that is real and
eternal. Christian Science is irrevocable — unpierced
27 by bold conjecture's sharp point, by bald philosophy, or
by man's inventions. It is divinely true, and every hour

in time and in eternity will witness more steadfastly to its   1
practical truth. And Science is not pantheism, but Christian Science.   3

Chief among the questions herein, and nearest my heart, is this: When shall Christianity be demonstrated according to Christ, in these words: "Neither shall they   6
say, Lo, here! or, lo there! for, behold, the kingdom of God is within you"?

EXHORTATION   9

Beloved brethren, the love of our loving Lord was never more manifest than in its stern condemnation of all error, wherever found. I counsel thee, rebuke and exhort one   12
another. Love all Christian churches for the gospel's sake; and be exceedingly glad that the churches are united in purpose, if not in method, to close the war between   15
flesh and Spirit, and to fight the good fight till God's will be witnessed and done on earth as in heaven.

Sooner or later all shall know Him, recognize the great   18
truth that Spirit is infinite, and find life in Him in whom we do "live, and move, and have our being" — life in Life, all in All. Then shall all nations, peoples, and   21
tongues, in the words of St. Paul, have "one God and Father of all, who is above all, and through all, and in you all." (Ephesians iv. 6.)   24

Have I wearied you with the mysticism of opposites? Truly there is no rest in them, and I have only traversed my subject that you may prove for yourselves the unsub-   27 stantial nature of whatever is unlike good, weigh a sigh, and rise into the rest of righteousness with its triumphant train.

Once more I write, Set your affections on things above; love one another; commune at the table of our Lord in one spirit; worship in spirit and in truth; and if daily adoring, imploring, and living the divine Life, Truth, Love, thou shalt partake of the bread that cometh down from heaven, drink of the cup of salvation, and be baptized in Spirit.

PRAYER FOR COUNTRY AND CHURCH

Pray for the prosperity of our country, and for her victory under arms; that justice, mercy, and peace continue to characterize her government, and that they shall rule all nations. Pray that the divine presence may still guide and bless our chief magistrate, those associated with his executive trust, and our national judiciary; give to our congress wisdom, and uphold our nation with the right arm of His righteousness.

In your peaceful homes remember our brave soldiers, whether in camp or in battle.[1] Oh, may their love of country, and their faithful service thereof, be unto them life-preservers! May the divine Love succor and protect them, as at Manila, where brave men, led by the dauntless Dewey, and shielded by the power that saved them, sailed victoriously through the jaws of death and blotted out the Spanish squadron.

Great occasion have we to rejoice that our nation, which

[1] This refers to the war between United States and Spain for the liberty of Cuba.

fed her starving foe, — already murdering her peaceful
seamen and destroying millions of her money, — will be
as formidable in war as she has been compassionate in
peace.

May our Father-Mother God, who in times past hath
spread for us a table in the wilderness and "in the midst
of our enemies," establish us in the most holy faith, plant
our feet firmly on Truth, the rock of Christ, the "substance
of things hoped for" — and fill us with the life and understanding of God, and good will towards men.

MARY BAKER EDDY

Message

to

The Mother Church

Boston, Massachusetts

June, 1900

Message
to
The Mother Church
Boston, Massachusetts

June, 1900

by

Mary Baker Eddy

Pastor Emeritus and Author of Science and Health
with Key to the Scriptures

Published by the
Trustees under the Will of Mary Baker G. Eddy
Boston, U.S.A.

Authorized Literature of
The First Church of Christ, Scientist
in Boston, Massachusetts

Message for 1900

MY beloved brethren, methinks even I am touched 1
with the tone of your happy hearts, and can see
your glad faces, aglow with gratitude, chinked within the 3
storied walls of The Mother Church. If, indeed, we may
be absent from the body and present with the ever-present
Love filling all space, time, and immortality — then I am 6
with thee, heart answering to heart, and mine to thine in
the glow of divine reflection.

I am grateful to say that in the last year of the nine- 9
teenth century this first church of our denomination,
chartered in 1879, is found crowned with unprecedented
prosperity; a membership of over sixteen thousand com- 12
municants in unity, with rapidly increasing numbers, rich
spiritual attainments, and right convictions fast forming
themselves into conduct. 15

Christian Science already has a hearing and following
in the five grand divisions of the globe; in Australia, the
Philippine Islands, Hawaiian Islands; and in most of the 18
principal cities, such as Boston, New York, Philadelphia,
Washington, Baltimore, Charleston, S. C., Atlanta, New
Orleans, Chicago, St. Louis, Denver, Salt Lake City, San 21
Francisco, Montreal, London, Edinburgh, Dublin, Paris,
Berlin, Rome, Pekin. Judging from the number of the
readers of my books and those interested in them, over a 24

[1]

1 million of people are already interested in Christian
Science; and this interest increases. Churches of this
3 denomination are springing up in the above-named cities,
and, thanks to God, the people most interested in this
old-new theme of redeeming Love are among the best people
6 on earth and in heaven.

The song of Christian Science is, "Work — work —
work — watch and pray." The close observer reports
9 three types of human nature — the right thinker and
worker, the idler, and the intermediate.

The right thinker works; he gives little time to society
12 manners or matters, and benefits society by his example
and usefulness. He takes no time for amusement, ease,
frivolity; he earns his money and gives it wisely to the
15 world.

The wicked idler earns little and is stingy; he has
plenty of means, but he uses them evilly. Ask how he
18 gets his money, and his satanic majesty is supposed to
answer smilingly: "By cheating, lying, and crime; his
dupes are his capital; his stock in trade, the wages of sin;
21 your idlers are my busiest workers; they will leave a
lucrative business to work for me." Here we add: The
doom of such workers will come, and it will be more sudden,
24 severe, and lasting than the adversary can hope.

The intermediate worker works at times. He says:
"It is my duty to take some time for myself; however, I
27 believe in working when it is convenient." Well, all that
is good. But what of the fruits of your labors? And he
answers: "I am not so successful as I could wish, but I
30 work hard enough to be so."

Now, what saith Christian Science? "When a man is right, his thoughts are right, active, and they are fruitful; he loses self in love, and cannot hear himself, unless he loses the chord. The right thinker and worker does his best, and does the thinking for the ages. No hand that feels not his help, no heart his comfort. He improves moments; to him time is money, and he hoards this capital to distribute gain."

If the right thinker and worker's servitude is duly valued, he is not thereby worshipped. One's idol is by no means his servant, but his master. And they who love a good work or good workers are themselves workers who appreciate a life, and labor to awake the slumbering capability of man. And what the best thinker and worker has said and done, they are not far from saying and doing. As a rule the Adam-race are not apt to worship the pioneer of spiritual ideas, — but ofttimes to shun him as their tormentor. Only the good man loves the right thinker and worker, and cannot worship him, for that would destroy this man's goodness.

To-day it surprises us that during the period of captivity the Israelites in Babylon hesitated not to call the divine name Yahwah, afterwards transcribed Jehovah; also that women's names contained this divine appellative and so sanctioned idolatry, — other gods. In the heathen conception Yahwah, misnamed Jehovah, was a god of hate and of love, who repented himself, improved on his work of creation, and revenged himself upon his enemies. However, the animus of heathen religion was not the incentive of the devout Jew — but has it not tainted the reli-

1 gious sects? This seedling misnomer couples love and
hate, good and evil, health and sickness, life and death,
3 with man — makes His opposites as real and normal as
the one God, and so unwittingly consents to many minds
and many gods. This precedent that would commingle
6 Christianity, the gospel of the New Testament and the
teaching of the righteous Galilean, Christ Jesus, with the
Babylonian and Neoplatonic religion, is being purged by
9 a purer Judaism and nearer approach to monotheism and
the perfect worship of one God.

To-day people are surprised at the new and forward
12 steps in religion, which indicate a renaissance greater than
in the mediæval period; but ought not this to be an agreeable surprise, inasmuch as these are progressive signs of
15 the times?

It should seem rational that the only perfect religion is
divine Science, Christianity as taught by our great Master;
18 that which leaves the beaten path of human doctrines and
is the truth of God, and of man and the universe. The
divine Principle and rules of this Christianity being de-
21 monstrable, they are undeniable; and they must be found
final, absolute, and eternal. The question as to religion
is: Does it demonstrate its doctrines? Do religionists
24 believe that God is *One* and *All?* Then whatever is real
must proceed from God, from Mind, and is His reflection
and Science. Man and the universe coexist with God in
27 Science, and they reflect God and nothing else. In divine
Science, divine Love includes and reflects all that really
is, all personality and individuality. St. Paul beautifully
30 enunciates this fundamental fact of Deity as the "Father

of all, who is above all, and through all, and in you all." 1
This scientific statement of the origin, nature, and government of all things coincides with the First Commandment 3
of the Decalogue, and leaves no opportunity for idolatry
or aught besides God, good. It gives evil no origin, no
reality. Here note the words of our Master corroborating 6
this as self-evident. Jesus said the opposite of God —
good — named devil — evil — "is a liar, and the father
of it" — that is, its origin is a myth, a lie. 9

Applied to Deity, Father and Mother are synonymous
terms; they signify one God. Father, Son, and Holy
Ghost mean God, man, and divine Science. God is self- 12
existent, the essence and source of the two latter, and their
office is that of eternal, infinite individuality. I see no
other way under heaven and among men whereby to have 15
one God, and man in His image and likeness, loving another as himself. This being the divine Science of divine
Love, it would enable man to escape from idolatry of 18
every kind, to obey the First Commandment of the Decalogue: "Thou shalt have no other gods before me;"
and the command of Christ: "Love thy neighbor as thy- 21
self." On this rock Christian Science is built. It may
be the rock which the builders reject for a season; but
it is the Science of God and His universe, and it will be- 24
come the head of the corner, the foundation of all systems
of religion.

The spiritual sense of the Scriptures understood enables 27
one to utilize the power of divine Love in casting out God's
opposites, called evils, and in healing the sick. Not mad-
ness, but might and majesty attend every footstep of 30

1 Christian Science. There is no imperfection, no lack in
the Principle and rules which demonstrate it. Only the
3 demonstrator can mistake or fail in proving its power and
divinity. In the words of St. Paul: "I count not myself
to have apprehended: but this one thing I do, forgetting
6 those things which are behind, and reaching forth to those
things which are before, I press toward the mark for the
prize of the high calling of God in Christ Jesus" — in the
9 true idea of God. Any mystery in Christian Science de-
parts when dawns the spiritual meaning thereof; and the
spiritual sense of the Scriptures is the scientific sense which
12 interprets the healing Christ. A child can measurably
understand Christian Science, for, through his simple faith
and purity, he takes in its spiritual sense that puzzles the
15 man. The child not only accepts Christian Science more
readily than the adult, but he practises it. This notable
fact proves that the so-called fog of this Science obtains
18 not in the Science, but in the material sense which the
adult entertains of it. However, to a man who uses tobacco, is profane, licentious, and breaks God's com-
21 mandments, that which destroys his false appetites and
lifts him from the stubborn thrall of sin to a meek and
loving disciple of Christ, clothed and in his right mind, is
24 not darkness but light.

Again, that Christian Science is the Science of God is
proven when, in the degree that you accept it, understand
27 and practise it, you are made better physically, morally,
and spiritually. Some modern exegesis on the prophetic
Scriptures cites 1875 as the year of the second coming of
30 Christ. In that year the Christian Science textbook,

"Science and Health with Key to the Scriptures," was 1
first published. From that year the United States official
statistics show the annual death-rate to have gradually 3
diminished. Likewise the religious sentiment has increased; creeds and dogmas have been sifted, and a
greater love of the Scriptures manifested. In 1895 it was 6
estimated that during the past three years there had been
more Bibles sold than in all the other 1893 years. Many
of our best and most scholarly men and women, distin- 9
guished members of the bar and bench, press and pulpit,
and those in all the walks of life, will tell you they never
loved the Bible and appreciated its worth as they did after 12
reading "Science and Health with Key to the Scriptures."
This is my great reward for having suffered, lived, and
learned, in a small degree, the Science of perfectibility 15
through Christ, the Way, the Truth, and the Life.

Is there more than one Christ, and hath Christ a second
appearing? There is but one Christ. And from ever- 18
lasting to everlasting this Christ is never absent. In doubt
and darkness we say as did Mary of old: "I know not
where they have laid him." But when we behold the 21
Christ walking the wave of earth's troubled sea, like Peter
we believe in the second coming, and would walk more
closely with Christ; but find ourselves so far from the em- 24
bodiment of Truth that ofttimes this attempt measurably
fails, and we cry, "Save, or I perish!" Then the tender,
loving Christ is found near, affords help, and we are saved 27
from our fears. Thus it is we walk here below, and wait
for the full appearing of Christ till the long night is past
and the morning dawns on eternal day. Then, if sin and 30

1 flesh are put off, we shall know and behold more nearly
the embodied Christ, and with saints and angels shall be
3 satisfied to go on till we awake in his likeness.

The good man imparts knowingly and unknowingly
goodness; but the evil man also exhales consciously and
6 unconsciously his evil nature — hence, be careful of your
company. As in the floral kingdom odors emit character-
istics of tree and flower, a perfume or a poison, so the hu-
9 man character comes forth a blessing or a bane upon
individuals and society. A wicked man has little real
intelligence; he may steal other people's good thoughts,
12 and wear the purloined garment as his own, till God's
discipline takes it off for his poverty to appear.

Our Master saith to his followers: "Bring forth things
15 new and old." In this struggle remember that sensitive-
ness is sometimes selfishness, and that mental idleness or
apathy is always egotism and animality. Usefulness is
18 doing rightly by yourself and others. We lose a percentage
due to our activity when doing the work that belongs to
another. When a man begins to quarrel with himself he
21 stops quarrelling with others. We must exterminate self
before we can successfully war with mankind. Then, at
last, the right will boil over the brim of life and the fire
24 that purifies sense with Soul will be extinguished. It is not
Science for the wicked to wallow or the good to weep.

Learn to obey; but learn first what obedience is.
27 When God speaks to you through one of His little ones,
and you obey the mandate but retain a desire to follow
your own inclinations, that is not obedience. I some-
30 times advise students not to do certain things which I

know it were best not to do, and they comply with my
counsel; but, watching them, I discern that this obedience
is contrary to their inclination. Then I sometimes withdraw that advice and say: "You may do it if you desire." But I say this not because it is the best thing to
do, but because the student is not willing — therefore,
not ready — to obey.

The secret of Christian Science in right thinking and
acting is open to mankind, but few, comparatively, see it;
or, seeing it, shut their eyes and wait for a more convenient
season; or as of old cry out: "Why art thou come hither
to torment me before the time?"

Strong desires bias human judgment and misguide action, else they uplift them. But the reformer continues
his lightning, thunder, and sunshine till the mental atmosphere is clear. The reformer must be a hero at all
points, and he must have conquered himself before he can
conquer others. Sincerity is more successful than genius
or talent.

The twentieth century in the ebb and flow of thought
will challenge the thinkers, speakers, and workers to do
their best. Whosoever attempts to ostracize Christian
Science will signally fail; for no one can fight against God,
and win.

My loyal students will tell you that for many years I
have desired to step aside and to have some one take my
place as leader of this mighty movement. Also that I
strove earnestly to fit others for this great responsibility.
But no one else has seemed equal to "bear the burden and
heat of the day."

1   Success in sin is downright defeat. Hatred bites the
heel of love that is treading on its head. All that worketh
3 good is some manifestation of God asserting and developing good. Evil is illusion, that after a fight vanisheth with
the new birth of the greatest and best. Conflict and perse-
6 cution are the truest signs that can be given of the greatness
of a cause or of an individual, provided this warfare is
honest and a world-imposed struggle. Such conflict never
9 ends till unconquerable right is begun anew, and hath
gained fresh energy and final victory.

Certain elements in human nature would undermine
12 the civic, social, and religious rights and laws of nations
and peoples, striking at liberty, human rights, and self-
government — and this, too, in the name of God, justice,
15 and humanity! These elements assail even the new-old
doctrines of the prophets and of Jesus and his disciples.
History shows that error repeats itself until it is extermi-
18 nated. Surely the wisdom of our forefathers is not added
but subtracted from whatever sways the sceptre of self and
pelf over individuals, weak provinces, or peoples. Here
21 our hope anchors in God who reigns, and justice and judgment are the habitation of His throne forever.

Only last week I received a touching token of unselfed
24 manhood from a person I never saw. But since publishing
this page I have learned it was a private soldier who sent
to me, in the name of a first lieutenant of the United States
27 infantry in the Philippine Islands, ten five-dollar gold
pieces snuggled in Pears' soap. Surely it is enough for a
soldier serving his country in that torrid zone to part with
30 his soap, but to send me some of his hard-earned money

cost me a tear! Yes, and it gave me more pleasure than 1
millions of money could have given.

Beloved brethren, have no discord over music. Hold 3
in yourselves the true sense of harmony, and this sense
will harmonize, unify, and unself you. Once I was pas-
sionately fond of material music, but jarring elements 6
among musicians weaned me from this love and wedded
me to spiritual music, the music of Soul. Thus it is with
whatever turns mortals away from earth to heaven; we 9
have the promise that "all things work together for good
to them that love God," — love good. The human sigh
for peace and love is answered and compensated by divine 12
love. Music is more than sound in unison. The deaf
Beethoven besieges you with tones intricate, profound,
commanding. Mozart rests you. To me his composition 15
is the triumph of art, for he measures himself against
deeper grief. I want not only quality, quantity, and variation in tone, but the unction of Love. Music is divine. 18
Mind, not matter, makes music; and if the divine tone be
lacking, the human tone has no melody for me. Adelaide
A. Proctor breathes my thought: — 21

> It flooded the crimson twilight
> Like the close of an angel's psalm,
> And it lay on my fevered spirit 24
> With a touch of infinite calm.

In Revelation St. John refers to what "the Spirit saith
unto the churches." His allegories are the highest criticism 27
on all human action, type, and system. His symbolic
ethics bravely rebuke lawlessness. His types of purity

1 pierce corruption beyond the power of the pen. They are
bursting paraphrases projected from divinity upon human-
3 ity, the spiritual import whereof "holdeth the seven stars
in His right hand and walketh in the midst of the seven
golden candlesticks" — the radiance of glorified Being.

6   In Revelation, second chapter, his messages to the
churches commence with the church of Ephesus. History
records Ephesus as an illustrious city, the capital of Asia
9 Minor. It especially flourished as an emporium in the
time of the Roman Emperor Augustus. St. Paul's life
furnished items concerning this city. Corresponding to
12 its roads, its gates, whence the Ephesian elders travelled to
meet St. Paul, led northward and southward. At the head
of the harbor was the temple of Diana, the tutelary divinity
15 of Ephesus. The earlier temple was burned on the night
that Alexander the Great was born. Magical arts pre-
vailed at Ephesus; hence the Revelator's saying: "I
18 have somewhat against thee, because thou hast left thy
first love . . . and will remove thy candlestick out of his
place, except thou repent." This prophecy has been ful-
21 filled. Under the influence of St. Paul's preaching the
magical books in that city were publicly burned. It were
well if we had a St. Paul to purge our cities of charlatanism.
24 During St. Paul's stay in that city — over two years — he
labored in the synagogue, in the school of Tyrannus, and
also in private houses. The entire city is now in ruins.

27   The Revelation of St. John in the apostolic age is symbolic, rather than personal or historical. It refers to the
Hebrew Balaam as the devourer of the people. Nicolaitan
30 church presents the phase of a great controversy, ready to

destroy the unity and the purity of the church. It is said
"a controversy was inevitable when the Gentiles entered
the church of Christ" in that city. The Revelator com-
mends the church at Ephesus by saying: "Thou hatest
the deeds of the Nicolaitanes, which I also hate." It is
written of this church that their words were brave and their
deeds evil. The orgies of their idolatrous feasts and their
impurities were part of a system supported by their doctrine and their so-called prophetic illumination. Their
distinctive feature the apostle justly regards as heathen,
and so he denounces the Nicolaitan church.

Alexander the Great founded the city of Smyrna, and
after a series of wars it was taken and sacked. The Revelator writes of this church of Smyrna: "Be thou faithful
unto death, and I will give thee a crown of life." A glad
promise to such as wait and weep.

The city of Pergamos was devoted to a sensual worship.
There Æsculapius, the god of medicine, acquired fame;
and a serpent was the emblem of Æsculapius. Its medical
practice included charms and incantations. The Revelator refers to the church in this city as dwelling "where
Satan's seat is." The Pergamene church consisted of the
school of Balaam and Æsculapius, idolatry and medicine.

The principal deity in the city of Thyatira was Apollo.
Smith writes: "In this city the amalgamation of different
pagan religions seems not to have been wholly discoun-
tenanced by the authorities of the Judæo-Christian
church."

The Revelator speaks of the angel of the church in
Philadelphia as being bidden to write the approval of this

1 church by our Master — he saith: "Thou hast a little
strength, and hast kept my word, and hast not denied my
3 name. Behold, I will make them of the synagogue of
Satan . . . to know that I have loved thee. . . . Hold
that fast which thou hast, that no man take thy crown."
6 He goes on to portray seven churches, the full number
of days named in the creation, which signifies a complete
time or number of whatever is spoken of in the Scriptures.
9 Beloved, let him that hath an ear (that discerneth spiritually) hear what the Spirit saith unto the churches; and
seek thou the divine import of the Revelator's vision —
12 and no other. Note his inspired rebuke to all the churches
except the church in Philadelphia — the name whereof
signifies "brotherly love." I call your attention to this
15 to remind you of the joy you have had in following the
more perfect way, or Golden Rule: "As ye would that
men should do to you, do ye." Let no root of bitterness
18 spring up among you, but hold in your full hearts fervently
the charity that seeketh not only her own, but another's
good. The angel that spake unto the churches cites Jesus
21 as "he that hath the key of David; that openeth and no
man shutteth, and shutteth and no man openeth;" in
other words, he that toiled for the spiritually indispensable.
24 At all times respect the character and philanthropy of
the better class of M.D.'s — and if you are stoned from
the pulpit, say in your heart as the devout St. Stephen said:
27 "Lord, lay not this sin to their charge."

When invited to a feast you naturally ask who are to be
the guests. And being told they are distinguished indi-
30 viduals, you prepare accordingly for the festivity. Putting

aside the old garment, you purchase, at whatever price, a 1
new one that is up to date. To-day you have come to a
sumptuous feast, to one that for many years has been await- 3
ing you. The guests are distinguished above human title
and this feast is a Passover. To sit at this table of their
Lord and partake of what divine Love hath prepared for 6
them, Christian Scientists start forward with true ambition. The Passover, spiritually discerned, is a wonderful
passage over a tear-filled sea of repentance — which of 9
all human experience is the most divine; and after this
Passover cometh victory, faith, and good works.

When a supercilious consciousness that saith "there is 12
no sin," has awakened to see through sin's disguise the
claim of sin, and thence to see that sin has no claim, it
yields to sharp conviction — it sits in sackcloth — it waits 15
in the desert — and fasts in the wilderness. But all this
time divine Love has been preparing a feast for this
awakened consciousness. To-day you have come to Love's 18
feast, and you kneel at its altar. May you have on a wed-
ding garment new and old, and the touch of the hem of
this garment heal the sick and the sinner! 21

In the words of St. John, may the angel of The Mother
Church write of this church: "Thou hast not left thy first
love, I know thy works, and charity, and service, and faith, 24
and thy patience, and thy works; and the last to be more
than the first."

<blockquote>
Watch! till the storms are o'er — 27
  The cold blasts done,
The reign of heaven begun,
  And love, the evermore. 30
</blockquote>

Message

to

The Mother Church
Boston, Massachusetts

June, 1901

Message
to
The Mother Church
Boston, Massachusetts

June, 1901

by

Mary Baker Eddy

Pastor Emeritus and Author of Science and Health
with Key to the Scriptures

Published by the
Trustees under the Will of Mary Baker G. Eddy
Boston, U.S.A.

Authorized Literature of
The First Church of Christ, Scientist
in Boston, Massachusetts

Message for 1901

BELOVED brethren, to-day I extend my heart-and- 1
hand-fellowship to the faithful, to those whose hearts
have been beating through the mental avenues of man- 3
kind for God and humanity; and rest assured you can
never lack God's outstretched arm so long as you are in
His service. Our first communion in the new century 6
finds Christian Science more extended, more rapidly advancing, better appreciated, than ever before, and nearer
the whole world's acceptance. 9

To-day you meet to commemorate in unity the life of
our Lord, and to rise higher and still higher in the individual consciousness most essential to your growth and 12
usefulness; to add to your treasures of thought the great
realities of being, which constitute mental and physical
perfection. The baptism of the Spirit, and the refresh- 15
ment and invigoration of the human in communion with
the Divine, have brought you hither.

All that is true is a sort of necessity, a portion of the 18
primal reality of things. Truth comes from a deep sincerity that must always characterize heroic hearts; it is
the better side of man's nature developing itself. 21

As Christian Scientists you seek to define God to your
own consciousness by feeling and applying the nature and
practical possibilities of divine Love: to gain the absolute 24

[1]

1 and supreme certainty that Christianity is now what Christ
Jesus taught and demonstrated — health, holiness, im-
3 mortality. The highest spiritual Christianity in individual
lives is indispensable to the acquiring of greater power in
the perfected Science of healing all manner of diseases.

6   We know the healing standard of Christian Science was
and is traduced by trying to put into the *old* garment the
new-old cloth of Christian healing. To attempt to twist
9 the fatal magnetic element of human will into harmony
with divine power, or to substitute good words for good
deeds, a fair seeming for right being, may suit the weak or
12 the worldly who find the standard of Christ's healing too
high for them. Absolute certainty in the practice of divine
metaphysics constitutes its utility, since it has a divine and
15 demonstrable Principle and rule — if some fall short of
Truth, others will attain it, and these are they who will
adhere to it. The feverish pride of sects and systems is
18 the death's-head at the feast of Love, but Christianity is
ever storming sin in its citadels, blessing the poor in spirit
and keeping peace with God.

21   What Jesus' disciples of old experienced, his followers
of to-day will prove, namely, that a departure from the
direct line in Christ costs a return under difficulties; dark-
24 ness, doubt, and unrequited toil will beset all their return-
ing footsteps. Only a firm foundation in Truth can give
a fearless wing and a sure reward.

27   The history of Christian Science explains its rapid
growth. In my church of over twenty-one thousand six
hundred and thirty-one communicants (two thousand four
30 hundred and ninety-six of whom have been added since

last November) there spring spontaneously the higher hope, 1
and increasing virtue, fervor, and fidelity. The special
benediction of our Father-Mother God rests upon this 3
hour: "Blessed are ye when men shall revile you, and persecute you, and shall say all manner of evil against you
falsely, for my sake." 6

GOD IS THE INFINITE PERSON

We hear it said the Christian Scientists have no God
because their God is not a person. Let us examine this. 9
The loyal Christian Scientists absolutely adopt Webster's
definition of God, "A Supreme Being," and the Standard
dictionary's definition of God, "The one Supreme Being, 12
self-existent and eternal." Also, we accept God, emphati-
cally, in the higher definition derived from the Bible, and
this accords with the literal sense of the lexicons: "God is 15
Spirit," "God is Love." Then, to define Love in divine
Science we use this phrase for God — divine Principle.
By this we mean Mind, a permanent, fundamental, intel- 18
ligent, divine Being, called in Scripture, Spirit, Love.

It is sometimes said: "God is Love, but this is no argument that Love is God; for God is light, but light is not 21
God." The first proposition is correct, and is not lost
by the conclusion, for Love expresses the nature of God;
but the last proposition does not illustrate the first, as 24
light, being matter, loses the nature of God, Spirit, deserts
its premise, and expresses God only in metaphor, therefore it is illogical and the conclusion is not properly drawn. 27
It is logical that because God is Love, Love is divine Prin-

1 ciple; then Love as either divine Principle or Person
stands for God — for both have the nature of God.
3 In logic the major premise must be convertible to the
minor.

In mathematics four times three is twelve, and three
6 times four is twelve. To depart from the rule of mathematics destroys the proof of mathematics; just as a departure from the Principle and rule of divine Science
9 destroys the ability to demonstrate Love according to
Christ, healing the sick; and you lose its susceptibility of
scientific proof.

12 God is the author of Science — neither man nor matter
can be. The Science of God must be, is, *divine*, predi-
cated of Principle and demonstrated as divine Love; and
15 Christianity is divine Science, else there is no Science and
no Christianity.

We understand that God is personal in a scientific
18 sense, but is not corporeal nor anthropomorphic. We understand that God is not finite; He is the infinite Person,
but not three persons in one person. Christian Scientists
21 are theists and monotheists. Those who misjudge us because we understand that God is the infinite One instead
of three, should be able to explain God's personality ra-
24 tionally. Christian Scientists consistently conceive of God
as One because He is infinite; and as triune, because He
is Life, Truth, Love, and these three are one in essence
27 and in office.

If in calling God "divine Principle," meaning divine
Love, more frequently than Person, we merit the epithet
30 "godless," we naturally conclude that he breaks faith with

his creed, or has no possible conception of ours, who be- 1
lieves that three persons are defined strictly by the word
Person, or as One; for if Person is God, and he believes 3
three persons constitute the Godhead, does not Person
here lose the nature of one God, lose monotheism, and
become less coherent than the Christian Scientist's sense 6
of Person as one divine infinite triune Principle, named in
the Bible Life, Truth, Love? — for each of these possesses
the nature of all, and God omnipotent, omnipresent, 9
omniscient.

Man is person; therefore divine metaphysics discrimi-
nates between God and man, the creator and the created, 12
by calling one the divine Principle of all. This suggests
another query: Do Christian Scientists believe in personality? They do, but their personality is defined spiritually, 15
not materially — by Mind, not by matter. We do not blot
out the material race of Adam, but leave all sin to God's
fiat — self-extinction, and to the final manifestation of the 18
real spiritual man and universe. We believe, according
to the Scriptures, that God is infinite Spirit or Person, and
man is His image and likeness: therefore man reflects 21
Spirit, not matter.

We are not transcendentalists to the extent of extin-
guishing anything that is real, good, or true; for God and 24
man in divine Science, or the logic of Truth, are coexistent
and eternal, and the nature of God must be seen in man,
who is His eternal image and likeness.   27

The theological God as a Person necessitates a creed
to explain both His person and nature, whereas God explains Himself in Christian Science. Is the human person, 30

1 as defined by Christian Science, more transcendental than
  theology's three divine persons, that live in the Father and
3 have no separate identity? Who says the God of theology
  is a Person, and the God of Christian Science is not a
  person, hence no God? Here is the departure. Person is
6 defined differently by theology, which reckons three as
  one and the infinite in a finite form, and Christian Science,
  which reckons one as one and this one *infinite*.

9   Can the infinite Mind inhabit a finite form? Is the God
  of theology a finite or an infinite Person? Is He one
  Person, or three persons? Who can conceive either of
12 three persons as one person, or of three infinites? We
  hear that God is not God except He be a Person, and this
  Person contains three persons: yet God must be One
15 although He is three. Is this pure, specific Christianity?
  and is God in Christian Science no God because He is not
  after this model of personality?

18   The logic of divine Science being faultless, its consequent
  Christianity is consistent with Christ's hillside sermon,
  which is set aside to some degree, regarded as impracticable
21 for human use, its theory even seldom named.

  God is Person in the infinite scientific sense of Him, but
  He can neither be one nor infinite in the corporeal or an-
24 thropomorphic sense.

  Our departure from theological personality is, that God's
  personality must be as infinite as Mind is. We believe in
27 God as the infinite Person; but lose all conceivable idea
  of Him as a finite Person with an infinite Mind. That
  God is either inconceivable, or is manlike, is not my sense
30 of Him. In divine Science He is "altogether lovely," and

consistently conceivable as the personality of infinite Love,   1
infinite Spirit, than whom there is none other.

Scholastic theology makes God manlike; Christian   3
Science makes man Godlike. The trinity of the Godhead
in Christian Science being Life, Truth, Love, constitutes
the individuality of the infinite Person or divine intelligence   6
called God.

Again, God being infinite Mind, He is the all-wise, all-
knowing, all-loving Father-Mother, for God made man in   9
His own image and likeness, and made them male and
female as the Scriptures declare; then does not our
heavenly Parent — the divine Mind — include within this   12
Mind the thoughts that express the different mentalities
of man and woman, whereby we may consistently say,
"Our Father-Mother God"? And does not this heavenly   15
Parent know and supply the differing needs of the individual mind even as the Scriptures declare He will?

Because Christian Scientists call their God "divine   18
Principle," as well as infinite Person, they have not taken
away their Lord, and know not where they have laid Him.
They do not believe there must be something tangible to   21
the personal material senses in order that belief may attend
their petitions to divine Love. The God whom all Christians now claim to believe in and worship cannot be con-   24
ceived of on that basis; He cannot be apprehended through
the material senses, nor can they gain any evidence of His
presence thereby. Jesus said, "Thomas, because thou   27
hast seen me, thou hast believed: blessed are they that
have not seen, and yet have believed."

Again I reiterate this cardinal point: There is but one
3 Christ, and Christ is divine — the Holy Ghost, or spiritual
idea of the divine Principle, Love. Is this scientific statement more transcendental than the belief of our brethren,
6 who regard Jesus as God and the Holy Ghost as the third
person in the Godhead? When Jesus said, "I and my
Father are one," and "my Father is greater than I," this
9 was said in the sense that one ray of light is light, and it
is one with light, but it is not the full-orbed sun. Therefore we have the authority of Jesus for saying Christ is not
12 God, but an impartation of Him.

Again: Is man, according to Christian Science, more
transcendental than God made him? Can he be too spir-
15 itual, since Jesus said, "Be ye therefore perfect, even as
your Father which is in heaven is perfect"? Is God
Spirit? He is. Then is man His image and likeness,
18 according to Holy Writ? He is. Then can man be material, or less than spiritual? As God made man, is he not
wholly spiritual? The reflex image of Spirit is not unlike
21 Spirit. The logic of divine metaphysics makes man none
too transcendental, if we follow the teachings of the
Bible.

24   The Christ was Jesus' spiritual selfhood; therefore
Christ existed prior to Jesus, who said, "Before Abraham
was, I am." Jesus, the only immaculate, was born of a
27 virgin mother, and Christian Science explains that mystic
saying of the Master as to his dual personality, or the spir-

itual and material Christ Jesus, called in Scripture the 1
Son of God and the Son of man — explains it as referring
to his eternal spiritual selfhood and his temporal man- 3
hood. Christian Science shows clearly that God is the
only generating or regenerating power.

The ancient worthies caught glorious glimpses of the 6
Messiah or Christ, and their truer sense of Christ baptized
them in Spirit — submerged them in a sense so pure it
made seers of men, and Christian healers. This is the 9
"Spirit of life in Christ Jesus," spoken of by St. Paul.
It is also the mysticism complained of by the rabbis, who
crucified Jesus and called him a "deceiver." Yea, it is 12
the healing power of Truth that is persecuted to-day, the
spirit of divine Love, and Christ Jesus possessed it, practised it, and taught his followers to do likewise. This 15
spirit of God is made manifest in the flesh, healing and saving men, — it is the Christ, Comforter, "which taketh away
the sin of the world;" and yet Christ is rejected of men! 18

The evil in human nature foams at the touch of good;
it crieth out, "Let us alone; what have we to do with
thee, . . . ? art thou come to destroy us? I know thee who 21
thou art; the Holy One of God." The Holy Spirit takes
of the things of God and showeth them unto the creature;
and these things being spiritual, they disturb the carnal 24
and destroy it; they are revolutionary, reformatory, and —
now, as aforetime — they cast out evils and heal the sick.
He of God's household who loveth and liveth most the 27
things of Spirit, receiveth them most; he speaketh wisely,
for the spirit of his Father speaketh through him; he
worketh well and healeth quickly, for the spirit giveth him 30

1 liberty: "Ye shall know the truth, and the truth shall
make you free."

3 Jesus said, "For all these things they will deliver you
up to the councils" and "If they have called the master
of the house Beelzebub, how much more shall they call
6 them of his household? Fear them not therefore: for
there is nothing covered, that shall not be revealed."

Christ being the Son of God, a spiritual, divine emana-
9 tion, Christ must be spiritual, not material. Jesus was
the son of Mary, therefore the son of man only in the
sense that man is the generic term for both male and
12 female. The Christ was not human. Jesus was human,
but the Christ Jesus represented both the divine and the
human, God and man. The Science of divine metaphysics
15 removes the mysticism that used to enthrall my sense of
the Godhead, and of Jesus as the Son of God and the son
of man. Christian Science explains the nature of God as
18 both Father and Mother.

Theoretically and practically man's salvation comes
through "the riches of His grace" in Christ Jesus. Divine
21 Love spans the dark passage of sin, disease, and death with
Christ's righteousness, — the atonement of Christ, whereby
good destroys evil, — and the victory over self, sin, disease,
24 and death, is won after the pattern of the mount. This is
working out our own salvation, for God worketh with us,
until there shall be nothing left to perish or to be pun-
27 ished, and we emerge gently into Life everlasting. This
is what the Scriptures demand — faith according to
works.

30 After Jesus had fulfilled his mission in the flesh as the

Son of man, he rose to the fulness of his stature in Christ, 1
the eternal Son of God, that never suffered and never
died. And because of Jesus' great work on earth, his dem- 3
onstration over sin, disease, and death, the divine nature
of Christ Jesus has risen to human apprehension, and we
see the Son of man in divine Science; and he is no longer 6
a material man, and mind is no longer in matter. Through
this redemptive Christ, Truth, we are healed and saved,
and that not of our selves, it is the gift of God; we are 9
saved from the sins and sufferings of the flesh, and are
the redeemed of the Lord.

THE CHRISTIAN SCIENTISTS' PASTOR   12

True, I have made the Bible, and "Science and Health
with Key to the Scriptures," the pastor for all the churches
of the Christian Science denomination, but that does not 15
make it impossible for this pastor of ours to preach! To
my sense the Sermon on the Mount, read each Sunday
without comment and obeyed throughout the week, would 18
be enough for Christian practice. The Word of God is a
powerful preacher, and it is not too spiritual to be practical, nor too transcendental to be heard and understood. 21
Whosoever saith there is no sermon without personal
preaching, forgets what Christian Scientists do not, namely,
that God is a Person, and that he should be willing to hear 24
a sermon from his personal God!

But, my brethren, the Scripture saith, "Answer not a
fool according to his folly, lest thou also be like unto him." 27
St. Paul complains of him whose god is his belly: to

1 such a one our mode of worship may be intangible, for it
is not felt with the fingers; but the spiritual sense drinks
3 it in, and it corrects the material sense and heals the sinning and the sick. If St. John should tell that man that
Jesus came neither eating nor drinking, and that he bap-
6 tized with the Holy Ghost and with fire, he would naturally reply, "That is too transcendental for me to believe,
or for my worship. That is Johnism, and only Johnites
9 would be seen in such company." But this is human: even
the word Christian was anciently an opprobrium; —
hence the Scripture, "When the Son of man cometh, shall
12 he find faith on the earth?"

Though a man were begirt with the Urim and Thum-
mim of priestly office, yet should not have charity, or should
15 deny the validity and permanence of Christ's command to
heal in all ages, he would dishonor that office and misin-
terpret evangelical religion. Divine Science is not an in-
18 terpolation of the Scriptures, it is redolent with health,
holiness, and love. It only needs the prism of divine
Science, which scholastic theology has obscured, to divide
21 the rays of Truth, and bring out the entire hues of God.
The lens of Science magnifies the divine power to human
sight; and we then see the allness of Spirit, therefore the
24 nothingness of matter.

NO REALITY IN EVIL OR SIN

Incorporeal evil embodies itself in the so-called corpo-
27 real, and thus is manifest in the flesh. Evil is neither
quality nor quantity: it is not intelligence, a person or a

principle, a man or a woman, a place or a thing, and God 1
never made it. The outcome of evil, called sin, is another
nonentity that belittles itself until it annihilates its own 3
embodiment: this is the only annihilation. The visible
sin should be invisible: it ought not to be seen, felt, or
acted: and because it ought not, we must know it is not, 6
and that sin is a lie from the beginning, — an illusion,
nothing, and only an assumption that nothing is something.
It is not well to maintain the position that sin is sin and 9
can take possession of us and destroy us, but well that we
take possession of sin with such a sense of its nullity as
destroys it. Sin can have neither entity, verity, nor power 12
thus regarded, and we verify Jesus' words, that evil, *alias*
devil, sin, is a lie — therefore is nothing and the father of
nothingness. Christian Science lays the axe at the root of 15
sin, and destroys it on the very basis of nothingness. When
man makes something of sin it is either because he fears it
or loves it. Now, destroy the conception of sin as some- 18
thing, a reality, and you destroy the fear and the love of
it; and sin disappears. A man's fear, unconquered, con-
quers him, in whatever direction. 21

In Christian Science it is plain that God removes the
punishment for sin only as the sin is removed — never
punishes it only as it is destroyed, and never afterwards; 24
hence the hope of universal salvation. It is a sense of sin,
and not a sinful soul, that is lost. Soul is immortal, but
sin is mortal. To lose the sense of sin we must first detect 27
the claim of sin; hold it invalid, give it the lie, and then
we get the victory, sin disappears, and its unreality is
proven. So long as we indulge the presence or believe in 30

1 the power of sin, it sticks to us and has power over us.
Again: To assume there is no reality in sin, and yet com-
3 mit sin, is sin itself, that clings fast to iniquity. The
Publican's wail won his humble desire, while the Phari-
see's self-righteousness crucified Jesus.

6 Do Christian Scientists believe that evil exists? We
answer, Yes and No! Yes, inasmuch as we do know
that evil, as a false claim, false entity, and utter falsity,
9 does exist in thought; and No, as something that enjoys,
suffers, or is *real*. Our only departure from ecclesiasticism on this subject is, that our faith takes hold of the
12 fact that evil cannot be made so real as to frighten us
and so master us, or to make us love it and so hinder our
way to holiness. We regard evil as a lie, an illusion,
15 therefore as unreal as a mirage that misleads the traveller
on his way home.

It is self-evident that error is not Truth; then it follows
18 that it is untrue; and if untrue, unreal; and if unreal, to
conceive of error as either right or real is sin in itself. To
be delivered from believing in what is unreal, from fear-
21 ing it, following it, or loving it, one must watch and pray
that he enter not into temptation — even as one guards
his door against the approach of thieves. Wrong is
24 thought before it is acted; you must control it in the first
instance, or it will control you in the second. To overcome all wrong, it must become unreal to us: and it is
27 good to know that wrong has no divine authority; therefore man is its master. I rejoice in the scientific apprehension of this grand verity.

30 The evil-doer receives no encouragement from my

declaration that evil is unreal, when I declare that he 1
must awake from his belief in this awful unreality, repent
and forsake it, in order to understand and demonstrate 3
its unreality. Error uncondemned is not nullified. We
must condemn the claim of error in every phase in order
to prove it false, therefore unreal. 6

The Christian Scientist has enlisted to lessen sin, disease, and death, and he overcomes them through Christ,
Truth, teaching him that they cannot overcome us. The 9
resistance to Christian Science weakens in proportion as
one understands it and demonstrates the Science of
Christianity. 12

A sinner ought not to be at ease, or he would never quit
sinning. The most deplorable sight is to contemplate the
infinite blessings that divine Love bestows on mortals, and 15
their ingratitude and hate, filling up the measure of
wickedness against all light. I can conceive of little short
of the old orthodox hell to waken such a one from 18
his deluded sense; for all sin is a deluded sense, and
dis-ease in sin is better than ease. Some mortals may
even need to hear the following thunderbolt of Jonathan 21
Edwards: —

"It is nothing but God's mere pleasure that keeps you
from being this moment swallowed up in everlasting de- 24
struction. He is of purer eyes than to bear to have you in
His sight. There is no other reason to be given why you
have not gone to hell since you have sat here in the house 27
of God, provoking His pure eyes by your sinful, wicked
manner of attending His solemn worship. Yea, there is
nothing else that is to be given as a reason why you do 30

1 not at this moment drop down into hell, but that God's
hand has held you up."

FUTURE PUNISHMENT OF SIN

My views of a future and eternal punishment take in a
poignant present sense of sin and its suffering, punishing
6 itself here and hereafter till the sin is destroyed. St.
John's types of sin scarcely equal the modern nonde-
scripts, whereby the demon of this world, its lusts, falsi-
9 ties, envy, and hate, supply sacrilegious gossip with the
verbiage of hades. But hatred gone mad becomes im-
becile — outdoes itself and commits suicide. Then let the
12 dead bury its dead, and surviving defamers share our pity.

In the Greek *devil* is named *serpent — liar — the
god of this world;* and St. Paul defines this world's god as
15 dishonesty, craftiness, handling the word of God deceit-
fully. The original text defines *devil* as *accuser,
calumniator;* therefore, according to Holy Writ these
18 qualities are objectionable, and ought not to proceed from
the individual, the pulpit, or the press. The Scriptures
once refer to an evil spirit as *dumb,* but in its origin evil
21 was loquacious, and was supposed to outtalk Truth and
to carry a most vital point. Alas! if now it is permitted
license, under sanction of the gown, to handle with gar-
24 rulity age and Christianity! Shall it be said of this century that its greatest discoverer is a woman to whom men
go to mock, and go away to pray? Shall the hope for our
27 race commence with one truth told and one hundred false-
hoods told about it?

The present self-inflicted sufferings of mortals from sin, 1
disease, and death should suffice so to awaken the suf-
ferer from the mortal sense of sin and mind in matter as 3
to cause him to return to the Father's house penitent and
saved; yea, quickly to return to divine Love, the author
and finisher of our faith, who so loves even the repentant 6
prodigal — departed from his better self and struggling
to return — as to meet the sad sinner on his way and to
welcome him home. 9

MEDICINE

Had not my first demonstrations of Christian Science
or metaphysical healing exceeded that of other methods, 12
they would not have arrested public attention and started
the great Cause that to-day commands the respect of our
best thinkers. It was that I healed the deaf, the blind, the 15
dumb, the lame, the last stages of consumption, pneumonia,
etc., and restored the patients in from one to three inter-
views, that started the inquiry, What is it? And when the 18
public sentiment would allow it, and I had overcome a
difficult stage of the work, I would put patients into the
hands of my students and retire from the comparative 21
ease of healing to the next more difficult stage of action
for our Cause.

From my medical practice I had learned that the dynam- 24
ics of medicine is Mind. In the highest attenuations of
homœopathy the drug is utterly expelled, hence it must
be mind that controls the effect; and this attenuation in 27
some cases healed where the allopathic doses would not.

1 When the "mother tincture" of one grain of the drug was
attenuated one thousand degrees less than in the beginning,
3 that was my favorite dose.

The weak criticisms and woeful warnings concerning
Christian Science healing are less now than were the
6 sneers forty years ago at the medicine of homœopathy;
and the medicine of Mind is more honored and respected
to-day than the old-time medicine of matter. Those who
9 laugh at or pray against transcendentalism and the Christian Scientist's religion or his medicine, should know the
danger of questioning Christ Jesus' healing, who admin-
12 istered no remedy apart from Mind, and taught his disciples none other. Christian Science seems transcendental
because the substance of Truth transcends the evidence
15 of the five personal senses, and is discerned only through
divine Science.

If God created drugs for medical use, Jesus and his
18 disciples would have used them and named them for that
purpose, for he came to do "the will of the Father." The
doctor who teaches that a human hypothesis is above a
21 demonstration of healing, yea, above the grandeur of our
great master Metaphysician's precept and example, and
that of his followers in the early centuries, should read
24 this Scripture: "The fool hath said in his heart, There is
no God."

The divine Life, Truth, Love — whom men call God —
27 is the Christian Scientists' healer; and if God destroys the
popular triad — sin, sickness, and death — remember it
is He who does it and so proves their nullity.

30   Christians and clergymen pray for sinners; they believe

that God answers their prayers, and that prayer is a divinely 1
appointed means of grace and salvation. They believe
that divine power, besought, is given to them in times of 3
trouble, and that He worketh with them to save sinners.
I love this doctrine, for I know that prayer brings the
seeker into closer proximity with divine Love, and thus 6
he finds what he seeks, the power of God to heal and to
save. Jesus said, "Ask, and ye shall receive;" and if not
immediately, continue to ask, and because of your often 9
coming it shall be given unto you; and he illustrated his
saying by a parable.

The notion that mixing material and spiritual means, 12
either in medicine or in religion, is wise or efficient, is
proven false. That animal natures give force to character
is egregious nonsense — a flat departure from Jesus' 15
practice and proof. Let us remember that the great Metaphysician healed the sick, raised the dead, and commanded even the winds and waves, which obeyed him 18
through spiritual ascendency alone.

MENTAL MALPRACTICE

From ordinary mental practice to Christian Science is a 21
long ascent, but to go from the use of inanimate drugs to
any susceptible misuse of the human mind, such as mesmerism, hypnotism, and the like, is to subject mankind 24
unwarned and undefended to the unbridled individual
human will. The currents of God flow through no such
channels. 27

The whole world needs to know that the milder forms

1 of animal magnetism and hypnotism are yielding to its
aggressive features. We have no moral right and no
3 authority in Christian Science for influencing the thoughts
of others, except it be to serve God and benefit mankind.
Man is properly self-governed, and he should be guided
6 by no other mind than Truth, the divine Mind. Christian
Science gives neither moral right nor might to harm either
man or beast. The Christian Scientist is alone with his
9 own being and with the reality of things. The mental
malpractitioner is not, cannot be, a Christian Scientist; he
is disloyal to God and man; he has every opportunity to
12 mislead the human mind, and he uses it. People may
listen complacently to the suggestion of the inaudible
falsehood, not knowing what is hurting them or that they
15 are hurt. This mental bane could not bewilder, darken, or
misguide consciousness, physically, morally, or spiritually,
if the individual knew what was at work and his power
18 over it.

This unseen evil is the sin of sins; it is never forgiven.
Even the agony and death that it must sooner or later
21 cause the perpetrator, cannot blot out its effects on himself till he suffers up to its extinction and stops practising
it. The crimes committed under this new-old *régime* of
24 necromancy or diabolism are not easily reckoned. At
present its mystery protects it, but its hidden modus and
flagrance will finally be known, and the laws of our land
27 will handle its thefts, adulteries, and murders, and will
pass sentence on the darkest and deepest of human
crimes.

30   Christian Scientists are not hypnotists, they are not

mortal mind-curists, nor faith-curists; they have faith, 1
but they have Science, understanding, and works as well.
They are not the *addenda*, the *et ceteras*, or new editions 3
of old errors; but they are what they are, namely, students of a demonstrable Science leading the ages.

QUESTIONABLE METAPHYSICS   6

In an article published in the *New York Journal*,
Rev. —— writes: "To the famous Bishop Berkeley of the
Church of England may be traced many of the ideas about 9
the spiritual world which are now taught in Christian
Science."

This clergyman gives it as his opinion that Christian 12
Science will be improved in its teaching and authorship
after Mrs. Eddy has gone. I am sorry for my critic, who
reckons hopefully on the death of an individual who loves 15
God and man; such foreseeing is not foreknowing, and
exhibits a startling ignorance of Christian Science, and a
manifest unfitness to criticise it or to compare its literature. 18
He begins his calculation erroneously; for Life is the
Principle of Christian Science and of its results. Death
is neither the predicate nor postulate of Truth, and Christ 21
came not to bring death but life into the world. Does this
critic know of a better way than Christ's whereby to benefit
the race? My faith assures me that God knows more 24
than any man on this subject, for did He not know all
things and results I should not have known Christian
Science, or felt the incipient touch of divine Love which 27
inspired it.

1 That God is good, that Truth is true, and Science is
Science, who can doubt; and whosoever demonstrates the
3 truth of these propositions is to some extent a Christian
Scientist. Is Science material? No! It is the Mind of
God — and God is Spirit. Is Truth material? No!
6 Therefore I do not try to mix matter and Spirit, since
Science does not and they will not mix. I am a spiritual
homœopathist in that I do not believe in such a compound.
9 Truth and Truth is not a compound; Spirit and Spirit is
not: but Truth and error, Spirit and matter, are compounds and opposites; so if one is true, the other is false.
12 If Truth is true, its opposite, error, is not; and if Spirit is
true and infinite, it hath no opposite; therefore matter
cannot be a reality.

15 I begin at the feet of Christ and with the numeration
table of Christian Science. But I do not say that one added
to one is three, or one and a half, nor say this to accom-
18 modate popular opinion as to the Science of Christianity.
I adhere to my text, that one and one are two all the way
up to the infinite calculus of the infinite God. The numer-
21 ation table of Christian Science, its divine Principle and
rules, are before the people, and the different religious
sects and the differing schools of medicine are discussing
24 them as if they understood its Principle and rules before
they have learned its numeration table, and insist that the
public receive their sense of the Science, or that it receive
27 no sense whatever of it.

Again: Even the numeration table of Christian Science
is not taught correctly by those who have departed from
30 its absolute simple statement as to Spirit and matter, and

that one and two are neither more nor less than three; 1
and losing the numeration table and the logic of Christian
Science, they have little left that the sects and faculties 3
can grapple. If Christian Scientists only would admit
that God is Spirit and infinite, yet that God has an opposite and that the infinite is not all; that God is good and 6
infinite, yet that evil exists and is real, — thence it would
follow that evil must either exist in good, or exist outside
of the *infinite*, — they would be in peace with the 9
schools.

This departure, however, from the scientific statement,
the divine Principle, rule, or demonstration of Christian 12
Science, results as would a change of the denominations
of mathematics; and you cannot demonstrate Christian
Science except on its fixed Principle and given rule, ac- 15
cording to the Master's teaching and proof. He was ultra;
he was a reformer; he laid the axe at the root of all error,
amalgamation, and compounds. He used no material 18
medicine, nor recommended it, and taught his disciples
and followers to do likewise; therefore he demonstrated
his power over matter, sin, disease, and death, as no other 21
person has ever demonstrated it.

Bishop Berkeley published a book in 1710 entitled
"Treatise Concerning the Principle of Human Knowl- 24
edge." Its object was to deny, on received principles of
philosophy, the reality of an external material world. In
later publications he declared physical substance to be 27
"only the constant relation between phenomena connected
by association and conjoined by the operations of the
universal mind, nature being nothing more than conscious 30

1 experience. Matter apart from conscious mind is an impossible and unreal concept." He denies the existence of
3 matter, and argues that matter is not *without* the mind, but within it, and that that which is generally called matter is only an impression produced by divine power on
6 the mind by means of invariable rules styled the laws of nature. Here he makes God the cause of all the ills of mortals and the casualties of earth.

9   Again, while descanting on the virtues of tar-water, he writes: "I esteem my having taken this medicine the greatest of all temporal blessings, and am convinced that
12 under Providence I owe my life to it." Making matter more potent than Mind, when the storms of disease beat against Bishop Berkeley's metaphysics and personality he
15 fell, and great was the fall — from divine metaphysics to tar-water!

     Christian Science is more than two hundred years old.
18 It dates beyond Socrates, Leibnitz, Berkeley, Darwin, or Huxley. It is as old as God, although its earthly advent is called the Christian era.

21   I had not read one line of Berkeley's writings when I published my work Science and Health, the Christian Science textbook.

24   In contradistinction to his views I found it necessary to follow Jesus' teachings, and none other, in order to demonstrate the divine Science of Christianity — the meta-
27 physics of Christ — healing all manner of diseases. Philosophy, *materia medica*, and scholastic theology were inadequate to prove the doctrine of Jesus, and I relin-
30 quished the form to attain the spirit or mystery of

godliness. Hence the mysticism, so called, of my writings   1
becomes clear to the godly.

Building on the rock of Christ's teachings, we have a   3
superstructure eternal in the heavens, omnipotent on earth,
encompassing time and eternity. The stone which the
builders reject is apt to be the cross, which they reject and   6
whereby is won the crown and the head of the corner.

A knowledge of philosophy and of medicine, the scho-
lasticism of a bishop, and the metaphysics (so called)   9
which mix matter and mind, — certain individuals call
aids to divine metaphysics, and regret their lack in my
books, which because of their more spiritual import heal   12
the sick! No Christly axioms, practices, or parables are
alluded to or required in such metaphysics, and the demonstration of matter minus, and God all, ends in some   15
specious folly.

The great Metaphysician, Christ Jesus, denounced all
such gilded sepulchres of his time and of all time. He   18
never recommended drugs, he never used them. What,
then, is our authority in Christianity for metaphysics based
on materialism? He demonstrated what he taught. Had   21
he taught the power of Spirit, and along with this the
power of matter, he would have been as contradictory
as the blending of good and evil, and the latter superior,   24
which Satan demanded in the beginning, and which has
since been avowed to be as real, and matter as useful, as
the infinite God, — good, — which, if indeed Spirit and   27
infinite, excludes evil and matter. Jesus likened such
self-contradictions to a kingdom divided against itself,
that cannot stand.   30

1   The unity and consistency of Jesus' theory and practice
give my tired sense of false philosophy and material the-
3 ology rest. The great teacher, preacher, and demonstrator
of Christianity is the Master, who founded his system of
metaphysics only on Christ, Truth, and supported it by
6 his words and deeds.

The five personal senses can have only a finite sense
of the infinite: therefore the metaphysician is sensual
9 that combines matter with Spirit. In one sentence he
declaims against matter, in the next he endows it with a
life-giving quality not to be found in God! and turns
12 away from Christ's purely spiritual means to the schools
and matter for help in times of need.

I have passed through deep waters to preserve Christ's
15 vesture unrent; then, when land is reached and the world
aroused, shall the word popularity be pinned to the seam-
less robe, and they cast lots for it? God forbid! Let
18 it be left to such as see God — to the pure in spirit,
and the meek that inherit the earth; left to them of a
sound faith and charity, the greatest of which is charity
21 — spiritual love. St. Paul said: "Though I speak
with the tongues of men and of angels, and have not
charity, I am become as sounding brass, or a tinkling
24 cymbal."

Before leaving this subject of the old metaphysicians,
allow me to add I have read little of their writings. I was
27 not drawn to them by a native or an acquired taste for
what was problematic and self-contradictory. What I
have given to the world on the subject of metaphysical
30 healing or Christian Science is the result of my own ob-

servation, experience, and final discovery, quite independ-   1
ent of all other authors except the Bible.

My critic also writes: "The best contributions that   3
have been made to the literature of Christian Science have
been by Mrs. Eddy's followers. I look to see some St.
Paul arise among the Christian Scientists who will inter-   6
pret their ideas and principles more clearly, and apply
them more rationally to human needs."

My works are the first ever published on Christian   9
Science, and nothing has since appeared that is correct
on this subject the basis whereof cannot be traced to some
of those works. The application of Christian Science is   12
healing and reforming mankind. If any one as yet has
healed hopeless cases, such as I have in one to three inter-
views with the patients, I shall rejoice in being informed   15
thereof. Or if a modern St. Paul could start thirty years
ago without a Christian Scientist on earth, and in this
interval number one million, and an equal number of sick   18
healed, also sinners reformed and the habits and appetites of mankind corrected, why was it not done? God is
no respecter of persons.   21

I have put less of my own personality into Christian
Science than others do in proportion, as I have taken out
of its metaphysics all matter and left Christian Science   24
as it is, purely spiritual, Christlike — the Mind of God
and not of man — born of the Spirit and not matter.
Professor Agassiz said: "Every great scientific truth goes   27
through three stages. First, people say it conflicts with
the Bible. Next, they say it has been discovered before.
Lastly, they say they had always believed it." Having   30

1 passed through the first two stages, Christian Science must
be approaching the last stage of the great naturalist's
3 prophecy.

It is only by praying, watching, and working for the
kingdom of heaven within us and upon earth, that we
6 enter the strait and narrow way, whereof our Master said,
"and few there be that find it."

Of the ancient writers since the first century of the
9 Christian era perhaps none lived a more devout Christian
life up to his highest understanding than St. Augustine.
Some of his writings have been translated into almost
12 every Christian tongue, and are classed with the choicest
memorials of devotion both in Catholic and Protestant
oratories.

15   Sacred history shows that those who have followed exclusively Christ's teaching, have been scourged in the
synagogues and persecuted from city to city. But this
18 is no cause for not following it; and my only apology for
trying to follow it is that I love Christ more than all the
world, and my demonstration of Christian Science in
21 healing has proven to me beyond a doubt that Christ,
Truth, is indeed the way of salvation from all that worketh or maketh a lie. As Jesus said: "It is enough for
24 the disciple that he be as his master." It is well to know
that even Christ Jesus, who was not popular among the
worldlings in his age, is not popular with them in this
27 age; hence the inference that he who would be popular
if he could, is not a student of Christ Jesus.

After a hard and successful career reformers usually
30 are handsomely provided for. Has the thought come to

Christian Scientists, Have we housed, fed, clothed, or visited a reformer for that purpose? Have we looked after or even known of his sore necessities? Gifts he needs not. God has provided the means for him while he was providing ways and means for others. But mortals in the advancing stages of their careers need the watchful and tender care of those who want to help them. The aged reformer should not be left to the mercy of those who are not glad to sacrifice for him even as he has sacrificed for others all the best of his earthly years.

I say this not because reformers are not loved, but because well-meaning people sometimes are inapt or selfish in showing their love. They are like children that go out from the parents who nurtured them, toiled for them, and enabled them to be grand coworkers for mankind, children who forget their parents' increasing years and needs, and whenever they return to the old home go not to help mother but to recruit themselves. Or, if they attempt to help their parents, and adverse winds are blowing, this is no excuse for waiting till the wind shifts. They should remember that mother worked and won for them by facing the winds. All honor and success to those who honor their father and mother. The individual who loves most, does most, and sacrifices most for the reformer, is the individual who soonest will walk in his footsteps.

To aid my students in starting under a tithe of my own difficulties, I allowed them for several years fifty cents on every book of mine that they sold. "With this percentage," students wrote me, "quite quickly we have regained our tuition for the college course."

1   Christian Scientists are persecuted even as all other
religious denominations have been, since ever the primi-
3 tive Christians, "of whom the world was not worthy."
We err in thinking the object of vital Christianity is only
the bequeathing of itself to the coming centuries. The
6 successive utterances of reformers are essential to its
propagation. The magnitude of its meaning forbids head-
long haste, and the consciousness which is most imbued
9 struggles to articulate itself.

Christian Scientists are practically non-resistants; they
are too occupied with doing good, observing the Golden
12 Rule, to retaliate or to seek redress; they are not quacks,
giving birth to nothing and death to all, — but they are
leaders of a reform in religion and in medicine, and they
15 have no craft that is in danger.

Even religion and therapeutics need regenerating.
Philanthropists, and the higher class of critics in theology
18 and *materia medica*, recognize that Christian Science
kindles the inner genial life of a man, destroying all lower
considerations. No man or woman is roused to the estab-
21 lishment of a new-old religion by the hope of ease, pleasure,
or recompense, or by the stress of the appetites and passions. And no emperor is obeyed like the man "clouting
24 his own cloak" — working alone with God, yea, like the
clear, far-seeing vision, the calm courage, and the great
heart of the unselfed Christian hero.

27   I counsel Christian Scientists under all circumstances
to obey the Golden Rule, and to adopt Pope's axiom:
"An honest, sensible, and well-bred man will not insult
30 me, and no other can." The sensualist and world-wor-

shipper are always stung by a clear elucidation of truth, 1
of right, and of wrong.

The only opposing element that sects or professions 3
can encounter in Christian Science is Truth opposed to
all error, specific or universal. This opposition springs
from the very nature of Truth, being neither personal nor 6
human, but divine. Every true Christian in the near
future will learn and love the truths of Christian Science
that now seem troublesome. Jesus said, "I came not to 9
send peace but a sword."

Has God entrusted me with a message to mankind? —
then I cannot choose but obey. After a long acquaintance 12
with the communicants of my large church, they regard
me with no vague, fruitless, inquiring wonder. I can use
the power that God gives me in no way except in the 15
interest of the individual and the community. To this
verity every member of my church would bear loving
testimony.   18

MY CHILDHOOD'S CHURCH HOME

Among the list of blessings infinite I count these dear:
Devout orthodox parents; my early culture in the Congre- 21
gational Church; the daily Bible reading and family
prayer; my cradle hymn and the Lord's Prayer, repeated
at night; my early association with distinguished Chris- 24
tian clergymen, who held fast to whatever is good, used
faithfully God's Word, and yielded up graciously what
He took away. It was my fair fortune to be often taught 27
by some grand old divines, among whom were the Rev.

1 Abraham Burnham of Pembroke, N. H., Rev. Nathaniel
Bouton, D. D., of Concord, N. H., Congregationalists;
3 Rev. Mr. Boswell, of Bow, N. H., Baptist; Rev. Enoch
Corser, and Rev. Corban Curtice, Congregationalists; and
Father Hinds, Methodist Elder. I became early a child
6 of the Church, an eager lover and student of vital Christianity. Why I loved Christians of the old sort was I
could not help loving them. Full of charity and good
9 works, busy about their Master's business, they had no
time or desire to defame their fellow-men. God seemed
to shield the whole world in their hearts, and they were
12 willing to renounce all for Him. When infidels assailed
them, however, the courage of their convictions was seen.
They were heroes in the strife; they armed quickly, aimed
15 deadly, and spared no denunciation. Their convictions
were honest, and they lived them; and the sermons their
lives preached caused me to love their doctrines.
18   The lives of those old-fashioned leaders of religion explain in a few words a good man. They fill the ecclesi-
astic measure, that to love God and keep His command-
21 ments is the whole duty of man. Such churchmen and
the Bible, especially the First Commandment of the Decalogue, and Ninety-first Psalm, the Sermon on the Mount,
24 and St. John's Revelation, educated my thought many
years, yea, all the way up to its preparation for and recep-
tion of the Science of Christianity. I believe, if those
27 venerable Christians were here to-day, their sanctified
souls would take in the spirit and understanding of Christian Science through the flood-gates of Love; with them
30 Love was the governing impulse of every action; their

piety was the all-important consideration of their being, 1
the original beauty of holiness that to-day seems to be
fading so sensibly from our sight. 3

To plant for eternity, the "accuser" or "calumniator"
must not be admitted to the vineyard of our Lord, and
the hand of love must sow the seed. Carlyle writes: 6
"Quackery and dupery do abound in religion; above all,
in the more advanced decaying stages of religion, they
have fearfully abounded; but quackery was never the 9
originating influence in such things; it was not the health
and life of religion, but their disease, the sure precursor
that they were about to die." 12

Christian Scientists first and last ask not to be judged
on a doctrinal platform, a creed, or a diploma for scientific
guessing. But they do ask to be allowed the rights of con- 15
science and the protection of the constitutional laws of
their land; they ask to be known by their works, to be
judged (if at all) by their works. We admit that they do 18
not kill people with poisonous drugs, with the lance, or
with liquor, in order to heal them. Is it for not killing
them thus, or is it for healing them through the might and 21
majesty of divine power after the manner taught by Jesus,
and which he enjoined his students to teach and practise,
that they are maligned? The richest and most positive 24
proof that a religion in this century is just what it was in
the first centuries is that the same reviling it received
then it receives now, and from the same motives which 27
actuate one sect to persecute another in advance of it.

Christian Scientists are harmless citizens that do not
kill people either by their practice or by preventing the 30

early employment of an M.D. Why? Because the effect
of prayer, whereby Christendom saves sinners, is quite
as salutary in the healing of all manner of diseases. The
Bible is our authority for asserting this, in both cases.
The interval that detains the patient from the attendance
of an M.D., occupied in prayer and in spiritual obedience
to Christ's mode and means of healing, cannot be fatal
to the patient, and is proven to be more pathological than
the M.D.'s material prescription. If this be not so, where
shall we look for the standard of Christianity? Have we
misread the evangelical precepts and the canonical writings of the Fathers, or must we have a new Bible and a
new system of Christianity, originating not in God, but
a creation of the schools — a material religion, proscrip-
tive, intolerant, wantonly bereft of the Word of God.

Give us, dear God, again on earth the lost chord of
Christ; solace us with the song of angels rejoicing with
them that rejoice; that sweet charity which seeketh not
her own but another's good, yea, which *knoweth no evil.*

Finally, brethren, wait patiently on God; return blessing for cursing; be not overcome of evil, but overcome
evil with good; be steadfast, abide and abound in faith,
understanding, and good works; study the Bible and the
textbook of our denomination; obey strictly the laws that
be, and follow your Leader only so far as she follows
Christ. Godliness or Christianity is a human necessity:
man cannot live without it; he has no intelligence, health,
hope, nor happiness without godliness. In the words of
the Hebrew writers: "Trust in the Lord with all thine
heart; and lean not unto thine own understanding. In

all thy ways acknowledge Him, and He shall direct thy 1
paths;" "and He shall bring forth thy righteousness as
the light, and thy judgment as the noonday." 3

The question oft presents itself, Are we willing to sacrifice self for the Cause of Christ, willing to bare our bosom
to the blade and lay ourselves upon the altar? Christian 6
Science appeals loudly to those asleep upon the hill-tops
of Zion. It is a clarion call to the reign of righteousness,
to the kingdom of heaven within us and on earth, and 9
Love is the way alway.

> O the Love divine that plucks us
>   From the human agony! 12
> O the Master's glory won thus,
>   Doth it dawn on you and me?
>
> And the bliss of blotted-out sin 15
>   And the working hitherto —
> Shall we share it — do we walk in
>   Patient faith the way thereto? 18

Message

to

The First Church of Christ Scientist

or

The Mother Church

Boston

June 15, 1902

Message

to
The First Church of Christ, Scientist
or
The Mother Church

Boston
June 15, 1902
by

Mary Baker Eddy

Pastor Emeritus and Author of Science and Health
with Key to the Scriptures

Published by the
Trustees under the Will of Mary Baker G. Eddy
Boston, U. S. A.

Message for 1902

THE OLD AND THE NEW COMMANDMENT

BELOVED brethren, another year of God's loving 1
providence for His people in times of persecution has
marked the history of Christian Science. With no special 3
effort to achieve this result, our church communicants
constantly increase in number, unity, steadfastness. Two
thousand seven hundred and eighty-four members have 6
been added to our church during the year ending June,
1902, making total twenty-four thousand two hundred and
seventy-eight members; while our branch churches are 9
multiplying everywhere and blossoming as the rose. Evil,
though combined in formidable conspiracy, is made to
glorify God. The Scripture declares, "The wrath of man 12
shall praise Thee: the remainder of wrath shalt Thou
restrain."

Whatever seems calculated to displace or discredit the 15
ordinary systems of religious beliefs and opinions wrestling only with material observation, has always met with
opposition and detraction; this ought not so to be, for 18
a system that honors God and benefits mankind should
be welcomed and sustained. While Christian Science,
engaging the attention of philosopher and sage, is circling 21

1 the globe, only the earnest, honest investigator sees
through the mist of mortal strife this daystar, and whither
3 it guides.

To live and let live, without clamor for distinction or
recognition; to wait on divine Love; to write truth first
6 on the tablet of one's own heart, — this is the sanity and
perfection of living, and my human ideal. The Science
of man and the universe, in contradistinction to all error,
9 is on the way, and Truth makes haste to meet and to welcome it. It is purifying all peoples, religions, ethics, and
learning, and making the children our teachers.

12 Within the last decade religion in the United States has
passed from stern Protestantism to doubtful liberalism.
God speed the right! The wise builders will build on the
15 stone at the head of the corner; and so Christian Science,
the little leaven hid in three measures of meal, — ethics,
medicine, and religion, — is rapidly fermenting, and en-
18 lightening the world with the glory of untrammelled truth.
The present modifications in ecclesiasticism are an outcome of progress; dogmatism, relegated to the past, gives
21 place to a more spiritual manifestation, wherein Christ
is Alpha and Omega. It was an inherent characteristic
of my nature, a kind of birthmark, to love the Church;
24 and the Church once loved me. Then why not remain
friends, or at least agree to disagree, in love, — part fair
foes. I never left the Church, either in heart or in doc-
27 trine; I but began where the Church left off. When the
churches and I round the gospel of grace, in the circle of
love, we shall meet again, never to part. I have always
30 taught the student to overcome evil with good, used no

other means myself; and ten thousand loyal Christian 1
Scientists to one disloyal, bear testimony to this fact.

The loosening cords of non-Christian religions in the 3
Orient are apparent. It is cause for joy that among the
educated classes Buddhism and Shintoism are said to
be regarded now more as a philosophy than as a religion. 6

I rejoice that the President of the United States has put
an end, at Charleston, to any lingering sense of the North's
half-hostility to the South, thus reinstating the old national 9
family pride and joy in the sisterhood of States.

Our nation's forward step was the inauguration of
home rule in Cuba, — our military forces withdrawing, 12
and leaving her in the enjoyment of self-government under
improved laws. It is well that our government, in its brief
occupation of that pearl of the ocean, has so improved her 15
public school system that her dusky children are learning
to read and write.

The world rejoices with our sister nation over the close 18
of the conflict in South Africa; now, British and Boer may
prosper in peace, wiser at the close than the beginning of
war. The dazzling diadem of royalty will sit easier on the 21
brow of good King Edward, — the muffled fear of death
and triumph canker not his coronation, and woman's
thoughts — the joy of the sainted Queen, and the lay of 24
angels — hallow the ring of state.

It does not follow that power must mature into oppression; indeed, right is the only real potency; and the only 27
true ambition is to serve God and to help the race. Envy
is the atmosphere of hell. According to Holy Writ, the
first lie and leap into perdition began with "Believe in 30

1 me." Competition in commerce, deceit in councils, dishonor in nations, dishonesty in trusts, begin with "Who
3 shall be greatest?" I again repeat, Follow your Leader,
only so far as she follows Christ.

I cordially congratulate our Board of Lectureship, and
6 Publication Committee, on their adequacy and correct
analysis of Christian Science. Let us all pray at this
Communion season for more grace, a more fulfilled life
9 and spiritual understanding, bringing music to the ear,
rapture to the heart — a fathomless peace between
Soul and sense — and that our works be as worthy as
12 our words.

My subject to-day embraces the First Commandment
in the Hebrew Decalogue, and the new commandment in
15 the gospel of peace, both ringing like soft vesper chimes
adown the corridors of time, and echoing and reechoing
through the measureless rounds of eternity.

18   GOD AS LOVE

The First Commandment, "Thou shalt have no other
gods before me," is a law never to be abrogated — a divine
21 statute for yesterday, and to-day, and forever. I shall
briefly consider these two commandments in a few of their
infinite meanings, applicable to all periods — past, present,
24 and future.

Alternately transported and alarmed by abstruse
problems of Scripture, we are liable to turn from them as
27 impractical, or beyond the ken of mortals, — and past
finding out. Our thoughts of the Bible utter our lives.

As silent night foretells the dawn and din of morn; as the 1
dulness of to-day prophesies renewed energy for to-morrow,
— so the pagan philosophies and tribal religions of yester- 3
day but foreshadowed the spiritual dawn of the twentieth
century — religion parting with its materiality.

Christian Science stills all distress over doubtful inter- 6
pretations of the Bible; it lights the fires of the Holy
Ghost, and floods the world with the baptism of Jesus.
It is this ethereal flame, this almost unconceived light of 9
divine Love, that heaven husbands in the First Commandment.

For man to be thoroughly subordinated to this com- 12
mandment, God must be intelligently considered and
understood. The ever-recurring human question and
wonder, What is God? can never be answered satisfac- 15
torily by human hypotheses or philosophy. Divine metaphysics and St. John have answered this great question
forever in these words: "God is Love." This absolute 18
definition of Deity is the theme for time and for eternity;
it is iterated in the law of God, reiterated in the gospel of
Christ, voiced in the thunder of Sinai, and breathed in 21
the Sermon on the Mount. Hence our Master's saying,
"Think not that I am come to destroy the law, or the
prophets: I am not come to destroy, but to fulfil." 24

Since God is Love, and infinite, why should mortals
conceive of a law, propound a question, formulate a doctrine, or speculate on the existence of anything which is 27
an antipode of *infinite* Love and the manifestation thereof?
The sacred command, "Thou shalt have no other gods
before me," silences all questions on this subject, and for- 30

1 ever forbids the thought of any other reality, since it is impossible to have aught unlike the infinite.

3   The knowledge of life, substance, or law, apart or other
than God — good — is forbidden. The curse of Love
and Truth was pronounced upon a lie, upon false knowl-
6 edge, the fruits of the flesh not Spirit. Since knowledge
of evil, of something besides God, good, brought death
into the world on the basis of a lie, Love and Truth de-
9 stroy this knowledge, — and Christ, Truth, demonstrated
and continues to demonstrate this grand verity, saving
the sinner and healing the sick. Jesus said a lie fathers
12 itself, thereby showing that God made neither evil nor its
consequences. Here all human woe is seen to obtain in
a false claim, an untrue consciousness, an impossible
15 creation, yea, something that is not of God. The Chris-
tianization of mortals, whereby the mortal concept and
all it includes is obliterated, lets in the divine sense of
18 being, fulfils the law in righteousness, and consummates
the First Commandment, "Thou shalt have no other gods
before me." All Christian faith, hope, and prayer, all
21 devout desire, virtually petition, Make me the image and
likeness of divine Love.

     Through Christ, Truth, divine metaphysics points the
24 way, demonstrates heaven here, — the struggle over, and
victory on the side of Truth. In the degree that man becomes spiritually minded he becomes Godlike. St. Paul
27 writes: "For to be carnally minded is death; but to be
spiritually minded is life and peace." Divine Science
fulfils the law and the gospel, wherein God is infinite Love,
30 including nothing unlovely, producing nothing unlike

Himself, the true nature of Love intact and eternal. Divine 1
metaphysics concedes no origin or causation apart from
God. It accords all to God, Spirit, and His infinite mani- 3
festations of love — man and the universe.

In the first chapter of Genesis, matter, sin, disease, and
death enter not into the category of creation or conscious- 6
ness. Minus this spiritual understanding of Scripture, of
God and His creation, neither philosophy, nature, nor
grace can give man the true idea of God — divine Love — 9
sufficiently to fulfil the First Commandment.

The Latin *omni*, which signifies *all*, used as an English
prefix to the words *potence, presence, science*, signifies all- 12
power, all-presence, all-science. Use these words to define
God, and nothing is left to consciousness but Love, without
beginning and without end, even the forever *I AM*, and 15
All, than which there is naught else. Thus we have
Scriptural authority for divine metaphysics — spiritual
man and the universe coexistent with God. No other 18
logical conclusion can be drawn from the premises,
and no other scientific proposition can be Christianly
entertained. 21

LOVE ONE ANOTHER

Here we proceed to another Scriptural passage which
serves to confirm Christian Science. Christ Jesus saith, 24
"A new commandment I give unto you, That ye love one
another; as I have loved you." It is obvious that he
called his disciples' special attention to his *new command-* 27
ment. And wherefore? Because it emphasizes the

1 apostle's declaration, "God is Love," — it elucidates
Christianity, illustrates God, and man as His likeness, and
3 commands man to love as Jesus loved.

The law and the gospel concur, and both will be fulfilled. Is it necessary to say that the likeness of God, Spirit,
6 is spiritual, and the likeness of Love is loving? When
loving, we learn that "God is Love;" mortals hating, or
unloving, are neither Christians nor Scientists. The new
9 commandment of Christ Jesus shows what true spirituality
is, and its harmonious effects on the sick and the sinner.
No person can heal or reform mankind unless he is actuated
12 by love and good will towards men. The coincidence between the law and the gospel, between the old and the new
commandment, confirms the fact that God and Love are
15 *one*. The spiritually minded are inspired with tenderness,
Truth, and Love. The life of Christ Jesus, his words and
his deeds, demonstrate Love. We have no evidence of
18 being Christian Scientists except we possess this inspiration, and its power to heal and to save. The energy that
saves sinners and heals the sick is divine: and Love is the
21 Principle thereof. Scientific Christianity works out the
rule of spiritual love; it makes man *active*, it prompts perpetual goodness, for the ego, or I, goes to the Father,
24 whereby man *is* Godlike. Love, purity, meekness, coexist in divine Science. Lust, hatred, revenge, coincide in
material sense. Christ Jesus reckoned man in Science,
27 having the kingdom of heaven within him. He spake of
man not as the offspring of Adam, a departure from God,
or His lost likeness, but as God's child. Spiritual love
30 makes man conscious that God is his Father, and the con-

sciousness of God as Love gives man power with untold 1
furtherance. Then God becomes to him the All-presence
— quenching sin; the All-power — giving life, health, 3
holiness; the All-science — all law and gospel.

Jesus commanded, "Follow me; and let the dead bury
their dead;" in other words, Let the world, popularity, 6
pride, and ease concern you less, and *love thou*. When
the full significance of this saying is understood, we shall
have better practitioners, and Truth will arise in human 9
thought with healing in its wings, regenerating mankind
and fulfilling the apostle's saying: "For the law of the
Spirit of life in Christ Jesus hath made me free from the 12
law of sin and death." Loving chords set discords in harmony. Every condition implied by the great Master,
every promise fulfilled, was loving and spiritual, urging 15
a state of consciousness that leaves the minor tones of so-
called material life and abides in Christlikeness.

The unity of God and man is not the dream of a heated 18
brain; it is the spirit of the healing Christ, that dwelt forever in the bosom of the Father, and should abide forever
in man. When first I heard the life-giving sound thereof, 21
and knew not whence it came nor whither it tended, it
was the proof of its divine origin, and healing power, that
opened my closed eyes. 24

Did the age's thinkers laugh long over Morse's discovery of telegraphy? Did they quarrel long with the
inventor of a steam engine? Is it cause for bitter com- 27
ment and personal abuse that an individual has met the
need of mankind with some new-old truth that counteracts
ignorance and superstition? Whatever enlarges man's 30

1 facilities for knowing and doing good, and subjugates
matter, has a fight with the flesh. Utilizing the capacities
3 of the human mind uncovers new ideas, unfolds spiritual
forces, the divine energies, and their power over matter,
molecule, space, time, mortality; and mortals cry out,
6 "Art thou come hither to torment us before the time?"
then dispute the facts, call them false or in advance of the
time, and reiterate, Let me alone. Hence the foot-
9 prints of a reformer are stained with blood. Rev. Hugh
Black writes truly: "The birthplace of civilization is not
Athens, but Calvary."

12   When the human mind is advancing above itself towards
the Divine, it is subjugating the body, subduing matter,
taking steps outward and upwards. This upward ten-
15 dency of humanity will finally gain the scope of Jacob's
vision, and rise from sense to Soul, from earth to heaven.

Religions in general admit that man becomes finally
18 spiritual. If such is man's ultimate, his predicate tending
thereto is correct, and inevitably spiritual. Wherefore,
then, smite the reformer who finds the more spiritual way,
21 shortens the distance, discharges burdensome baggage,
and increases the speed of mortals' transit from matter
to Spirit — yea, from sin to holiness? This is indeed our
24 sole proof that Christ, Truth, is the way. The old and
recurring martyrdom of God's best witnesses is the in-
firmity of evil, the *modus operandi* of human error,
27 carnality, opposition to God and His power in man.
Persecuting a reformer is like sentencing a man for com-
municating with foreign nations in other ways than by
30 walking every step over the land route, and swimming the

ocean with a letter in his hand to leave on a foreign shore. 1
Our heavenly Father never destined mortals who seek
for a better country to wander on the shores of time dis- 3
appointed travellers, tossed to and fro by adverse circumstances, inevitably subject to sin, disease, and death.
Divine Love waits and pleads to save mankind — and 6
awaits with warrant and welcome, grace and glory, the
earth-weary and heavy-laden who find and point the path
to heaven. 9

Envy or abuse of him who, having a new idea or a more
spiritual understanding of God, hastens to help on his
fellow-mortals, is neither Christian nor Science. If a 12
postal service, a steam engine, a submarine cable, a wire-
less telegraph, each in turn has helped mankind, how
much more is accomplished when the race is helped on- 15
ward by a new-old message from God, even the knowledge of salvation from sin, disease, and death.

The world's wickedness gave our glorified Master a 18
bitter cup — which he drank, giving thanks, then gave
it to his followers to drink. Therefore it is thine, advancing Christian, and this is thy Lord's benediction upon 21
it: "Blessed are ye, when men shall revile you, and persecute you, and shall say all manner of evil against you
falsely, for my sake. Rejoice, and be exceeding glad: 24
for great is your reward in heaven: for so persecuted they
the prophets which were before you."

Of old the Jews put to death the Galilean Prophet, the 27
best Christian on earth, for the truths he said and did:
while to-day Jew and Christian can unite in doctrine and in
practice on the very basis of his words and works. The Jew 30

1 believes that the Messiah or the Christ has not yet come;
the Christian believes that Christ is come and is God.
3 Here Christian Science intervenes, explains these doctrinal
points, cancels the disagreement, and settles the whole question on the basis that Christ is the Messiah, the true spir-
6 itual idea, and this ideal of God is *now* and *forever*, *here* and
everywhere. The Jew who believes in the First Commandment is a monotheist, he has one omnipresent God: thus
9 the Jew unites with the Christian idea that God is come,
and is ever present. The Christian who believes in the
First Commandment is a monotheist: thus he virtually
12 unites with the Jew's belief in one God, and that Jesus
Christ is not God, as he himself declared, but is the Son of
God. This declaration of Christ, understood, conflicts not
15 at all with another of his sayings: "I and my Father are
one," — that is, one in quality, not in quantity. As a drop
of water is one with the ocean, a ray of light one with the
18 sun, even so God and man, Father and son, are one in
being. The Scripture reads: "For in Him we live, and
move, and have our being."

21   Here allow me to interpolate some matters of business
that ordinarily find no place in my Message. It is a privilege to acquaint communicants with the financial transac-
24 tions of this church, so far as I know them, and especially
before making another united effort to purchase more land
and enlarge our church edifice so as to seat the large number
27 who annually favor us with their presence on Communion
Sunday.

When founding the institutions and early movements of
30 the Cause of Christian Science, I furnished the money from

my own private earnings to meet the expenses involved. 1
In this endeavor self was forgotten, peace sacrificed, Christ
and our Cause my only incentives, and each success in- 3
curred a sharper fire from enmity.

During the last seven years I have transferred to The
Mother Church, of my personal property and funds, to the 6
value of about one hundred and twenty thousand dollars;
and the net profits from the business of The Christian Science Publishing Society (which was a part of this transfer) 9
yield this church a liberal income. I receive no personal
benefit therefrom except the privilege of publishing my
books in their publishing house, and desire none other. 12

The land on which to build The First Church of Christ,
Scientist, in Boston, had been negotiated for, and about one
half the price paid, when a loss of funds occurred, and I 15
came to the rescue, purchased the mortgage on the lot
corner of Falmouth and Caledonia (now Norway) Streets;
paying for it the sum of $4,963.50 and interest, through my 18
legal counsel. After the mortgage had expired and the note
therewith became due, legal proceedings were instituted by
my counsel advertising the property in the Boston news- 21
papers, and giving opportunity for those who had previously
negotiated for the property to redeem the land by paying
the amount due on the mortgage. But no one offering 24
the price I had paid for it, nor to take the property off my
hands, the mortgage was foreclosed, and the land legally
conveyed to me, by my counsel. This land, now valued at 27
twenty thousand dollars, I afterwards gave to my church
through trustees, who were to be known as "The Christian
Science Board of Directors." A copy of this deed is pub- 30

1 lished in our Church Manual. About five thousand dollars
had been paid on the land when I redeemed it. The only
3 interest I retain in this property is to save it for my church.
I can neither rent, mortgage, nor sell this church edifice nor
the land whereon it stands.

6   I suggest as a motto for every Christian Scientist, — a
living and life-giving spiritual shield against the powers of
darkness, —

9   "Great not like Cæsar, stained with blood,
                  But only great as I am good."

The only genuine success possible for any Christian — and
12 the only success I have ever achieved — has been accomplished on this solid basis. The remarkable growth and
prosperity of Christian Science are its legitimate fruit. A
15 successful end could never have been compassed on any
other foundation, — with truths so counter to the common
convictions of mankind to present to the world. From the
18 beginning of the great battle every forward step has been
met (not by mankind, but by a kind of men) with mockery,
envy, rivalry, and falsehood—as achievement after achieve-
21 ment has been blazoned on the forefront of the world and
recorded in heaven. The popular philosophies and religions have afforded me neither favor nor protection in the
24 great struggle. Therefore, I ask: What has shielded and
prospered preeminently our great Cause, but the outstretched arm of infinite Love? This pregnant question,
27 answered frankly and honestly, should forever silence all
private criticisms, all unjust public aspersions, and afford
an open field and fair play.

In the eighties, anonymous letters mailed to me contained threats to blow up the hall where I preached; yet I never lost my faith in God, and neither informed the police of these letters nor sought the protection of the laws of my country. I leaned on God, and was safe.

Healing all manner of diseases without charge, keeping a free institute, rooming and boarding indigent students that I taught "without money and without price," I struggled on through many years; and while dependent on the income from the sale of Science and Health, my publisher paid me not one dollar of royalty on its first edition. Those were days wherein the connection between justice and being approached the mythical. Before entering upon my great life-work, my income from literary sources was ample, until, declining dictation as to what I should write, I became poor for Christ's sake. My husband, Colonel Glover, of Charleston, South Carolina, was considered wealthy, but much of his property was in slaves, and I declined to sell them at his decease in 1844, for I could never believe that a human being was my property.

Six weeks I waited on God to suggest a name for the book I had been writing. Its title, Science and Health, came to me in the silence of night, when the steadfast stars watched over the world, — when slumber had fled, — and I rose and recorded the hallowed suggestion. The following day I showed it to my literary friends, who advised me to drop both the book and the title. To this, however, I gave no heed, feeling sure that God had led me to write that book, and had whispered that name to my waiting hope and prayer. It was to me the "still, small voice" that came to

1 Elijah after the earthquake and the fire. Six months there-
after Miss Dorcas Rawson of Lynn brought to me Wyclif's
3 translation of the New Testament, and pointed out that
identical phrase, "Science and Health," which is rendered
in the Authorized Version "knowledge of salvation."
6 This was my first inkling of Wyclif's use of that combina-
tion of words, or of their rendering. To-day I am the happy
possessor of a copy of Wyclif, the invaluable gift of two
9 Christian Scientists, — Mr. W. Nicholas Miller, K.C., and
Mrs. F. L. Miller, of London, England.

GODLIKENESS

12   St. Paul writes: "Follow peace with all men, and holiness, without which no man shall see the Lord." To attain
peace and holiness is to recognize the divine presence and
15 allness. Jesus said: "I am the way." Kindle the watch-
fires of unselfed love, and they throw a light upon the un-
complaining agony in the life of our Lord; they open the
18 enigmatical seals of the angel, standing in the sun, a glorified spiritual idea of the ever-present God — in whom there
is no darkness, but all is light, and man's immortal being.
21 The meek might, sublime patience, wonderful works, and
opening not his mouth in self-defense against false witnesses, express the life of Godlikeness. Fasting, feasting,
24 or penance, — merely outside forms of religion, — fail to
elucidate Christianity: they reach not the heart nor reno-
vate it; they never destroy one iota of hypocrisy, pride,
27 self-will, envy, or hate. The mere form of godliness,

coupled with selfishness, worldliness, hatred, and lust, are   1
knells tolling the burial of Christ.

Jesus said, "If ye love me, keep my commandments."   3
He knew that obedience is the test of love; that one gladly
obeys when obedience gives him happiness. Selfishly, or
otherwise, all are ready to seek and obey what they love.   6
When mortals learn to love aright; when they learn that
man's highest happiness, that which has most of heaven in
it, is in blessing others, and self-immolation — they will   9
obey both the old and the new commandment, and receive
the reward of obedience.

Many sleep who should keep themselves awake and   12
waken the world. Earth's actors change earth's scenes;
and the curtain of human life should be lifted on reality, on
that which outweighs time; on duty done and life perfected,   15
wherein joy is real and fadeless. Who of the world's lovers
ever found her true? It is wise to be willing to wait on God,
and to be wiser than serpents; to hate no man, to love one's   18
enemies, and to square accounts with each passing hour.
Then thy gain outlives the sun, for the sun shines but to
show man the beauty of holiness and the wealth of love.   21
Happiness consists in being and in doing good; only what
God gives, and what we give ourselves and others through
His tenure, confers happiness: conscious worth satisfies   24
the hungry heart, and nothing else can. Consult thy every-
day life; take its answer as to thy aims, motives, fondest
purposes, and this oracle of years will put to flight all care   27
for the world's soft flattery or its frown. Patience and res-
ignation are the pillars of peace that, like the sun beneath
the horizon, cheer the heart susceptible of light with prom-   30

1 ised joy. Be faithful at the temple gate of conscience,
wakefully guard it; then thou wilt know when the thief
3 cometh.

The constant spectacle of sin thrust upon the pure sense
of the immaculate Jesus made him a man of sorrows. He
6 lived when mortals looked ignorantly, as now, on the might
of divine power manifested through man; only to mock,
wonder, and perish. Sad to say, the cowardice and self-
9 seeking of his disciples helped crown with thorns the life of
him who broke not the bruised reed and quenched not the
smoking flax, — who caused not the feeble to fall, nor
12 spared through false pity the consuming tares. Jesus was
compassionate, true, faithful to rebuke, ready to forgive.
He said, "Inasmuch as ye have done it unto one of the
15 least of these my brethren, ye have done it unto me."
"Love one another, as I have loved you." No estrange-
ment, no emulation, no deceit, enters into the heart that
18 loves as Jesus loved. It is a false sense of love that, like
the summer brook, soon gets dry. Jesus laid down his life
for mankind; what more could he do? Beloved, how much
21 of what he did are we doing? Yet he said, "The works
that I do shall he do." When this prophecy of the great
Teacher is fulfilled we shall have more effective healers and
24 less theorizing; faith without proof loses its life, and it
should be buried. The ignoble conduct of his disciples
towards their Master, showing their unfitness to follow
27 him, ended in the downfall of genuine Christianity, about
the year 325, and the violent death of all his disciples save
one.

30   The nature of Jesus made him keenly alive to the

injustice, ingratitude, treachery, and brutality that he 1
received. Yet behold his love! So soon as he burst the
bonds of the tomb he hastened to console his unfaithful 3
followers and to disarm their fears. Again: True to his
divine nature, he rebuked them on the eve of his ascension,
called one a "fool" — then, lifting up his hands and bless- 6
ing them, he rose from earth to heaven.

The Christian Scientist cherishes no resentment; he
knows that that would harm him more than all the malice 9
of his foes. Brethren, even as Jesus forgave, forgive thou.
I say it with joy, — no person can commit an offense
against me that I cannot forgive. Meekness is the armor 12
of a Christian, his shield and his buckler. He entertains
angels who listens to the lispings of repentance seen in a
tear — happier than the conqueror of a world. To the 15
burdened and weary, Jesus saith: "Come unto me."
O glorious hope! there remaineth a rest for the righteous,
a rest in Christ, a peace in Love. The thought of it stills 18
complaint; the heaving surf of life's troubled sea foams
itself away, and underneath is a deep-settled calm.

Are earth's pleasures, its ties and its treasures, taken 21
away from you? It is divine Love that doeth it, and
sayeth, "Ye have need of all these things." A danger
besets thy path? — a spiritual behest, in reversion, awaits 24
you.

The great Master triumphed in furnace fires. Then,
Christian Scientists, trust, and trusting, you will find divine 27
Science glorifies the cross and crowns the association with
our Saviour in his life of love. There is no redundant
drop in the cup that our Father permits us. Christ 30

1 walketh over the wave; on the ocean of events, mounting
the billow or going down into the deep, the voice of him
3 who stilled the tempest saith, "It is I; be not afraid."
Thus he bringeth us into the desired haven, the kingdom
of Spirit; and the hues of heaven, tipping the dawn of
6 everlasting day, joyfully whisper, "No drunkards within,
no sorrow, no pain; and the glory of earth's woes is risen
upon you, rewarding, satisfying, glorifying thy unfaltering
9 faith and good works with the fulness of divine Love."

> 'T was God who gave that word of might
> Which swelled creation's lay, —
> 12   "Let there be light, and there was light," —
> That swept the clouds away;
> 'T was Love whose finger traced aloud
> 15   A bow of promise on the cloud.

Beloved brethren, are you ready to join me in this proposition, namely, in 1902 to begin omitting our *annual*
18 gathering at Pleasant View, — thus breaking any seeming
connection between the sacrament in our church and a
pilgrimage to Concord? I shall be the loser by this change,
21 for it gives me great joy to look into the faces of my dear
church-members; but in this, as all else, I can bear the
cross, while gratefully appreciating the privilege of meet-
24 ing you all *occasionally* in the metropolis of my native
State, whose good people welcome Christian Scientists.

THE · PLIMPTON · PRESS
NORWOOD · MASS · U · S · A